Timber
A Call to Personal and Corporate Renewal

TIMBER

A Call to Personal and Corporate Renewal

REG ANDREWS

Foreword by Charles Price

Essence PUBLISHING

Belleville, Ontario, Canada

TIMBER
Copyright © 2007, Reg Andrews

Cover Photograph by Harold Andrews

ISBN: 978-1-55452-224-8

**For more information and/or to order
additional copies of Timber and Timber Study Guide,
please contact:**
SummitPublications.org
info@summitpublications.org

Essence Publishing is a Christian Book Publisher dedicated to furthering the work of Christ through the written word. For more information, contact: 20 Hanna Court, Belleville, Ontario, Canada K8P 5J2.
Phone: 1-800-238-6376. Fax: (613) 962-3055.
E-mail: info@essence-publishing.com
Web site: www.essence-publishing.com

Printed in Canada
by

Essence
PUBLISHING

To my sons, Kent and Brad—each a rich blessing in
my life—who
give me hope for tomorrow's Church.

Table of Contents

Foreword

MOST CHRISTIANS LOVE THE IDEA OF SPIRITUAL revival. We enjoy reading stories of God working in remarkable ways, reviving His Church, ushering new people into the kingdom of God, resulting in Christians taking the gospel to the world with newfound confidence and boldness. Such stories stir our hearts, whet our appetites, and cause us to long that God may do it again in our own day. This longing speaks of health in our souls and faith in our hearts. But there is often a vitally overlooked ingredient—and it is here we balk and take a second thought. There is a price to pay! It is not a purchase price that obligates God to work, for all His dealings with us are on the basis of His free, unearned kindness and grace. But it is the price of unrelenting submission of our lives to Christ and operating exclusively on His terms.

The key to this book is God's word to Haggai to "*Go up into the mountains and bring down timber and build the house*" (Haggai 1:8). Reg Andrews creatively explores mountains in Scripture where God moulded and equipped people for new expressions of His purpose. Whether about Abraham on Mount Moriah, Moses on Mount Sinai, Elijah on Mount Carmel, or Christ

Himself on Mount Calvary, these timeless stories teach us forcibly what kind of "timber" equips us to be effective agents of God in our world and to live in the centre of His purposes. The warm anecdotes, memories of childhood experiences in Newfoundland, and experiences of God's enabling in varied but fruitful ministry leading up to the writer's years as executive pastor of The Peoples Church in Toronto all explain, enhance, and illustrate these truths for our day.

In the years I have been a colleague of Reg Andrews, I have seen the heart and spirit that come out in this book expressed and demonstrated. I pray it will ignite a new flame in the hearts of many of us so that we, too, will be willing to climb the mountains and *"bring down timber and build [God's] house,"* resulting in fresh power, holiness, and fruitfulness.

Charles Price
The Peoples Church, Toronto

Preface

A S I INTERACT WITH BELIEVERS MY AGE (FIFTY-SOME-thing) and older, I sense a collective desire that runs deep into our souls—the desire to see the Church in our nation revived. We lament the moral and spiritual decline that characterizes our land—the success of the "progressive" liberal agenda in the development of public policy and the expulsion of Christian values from our education systems and social structures. The steady push of the anti-Christian forces in our world has resulted in not just a post-Christian era but, more accurately, an anti-Christian era. The only hope now of seeing the tide turn and of experiencing societal transformation, which we know is essential, is to witness a visitation of God to His Church in a manner our generation has not seen. This book is written out of a desire to see such renewal in the Church of Jesus Christ.

In support of the values I want to highlight as I examine the basics of Christian faith and life, I have chosen to integrate anecdotes from my childhood, growing up in a pastor's home in rural Newfoundland. It was in that setting that I met Jesus and it was in that setting that the spiritual foundation stones of my life were laid. It was in that setting that Christian essentials were forged in my heart and mind. My hope is that the perspectives gained through an honest review of the insights derived from those experiences as well as some of my later adventures with God will help bring clarity to the issues I will be addressing.

In Newfoundland in the late sixties, high school students were required to write provincial exams. Knowing that your final grade was going to be assigned by an educator whom you'd never seen (more importantly, who'd never seen you) brought a high degree of tension to the exam room. These exams were implemented from grade 9 on, so it was at the end of the ninth grade that I learned the meaning of the term *invigilator*. The invigilator was the teacher responsible for the supervision of the exam room, ensuring that the stringent rules applicable to all exam rooms throughout the province were adhered to. I well remember watching the clock at the front of the gymnasium as I would near the end of the examination period. "Ten minutes remaining," an alert from the invigilator, would often engender minor panic as I realized that what was to be accomplished in the next ten minutes could well determine whether my grade would be subpar, acceptable, or above average. I needed to review my answers, fill in any empty blanks, and do my absolute best to leave no stone unturned in ensuring that my answers were accurate and complete. I, more often than not, would hope that there would be extra grace granted from the heart of the invigilator and some extra discretionary time awarded.

I acknowledge that what I'm feeling regarding the Church may well be the result of being especially aware, as I was in the exam room, that time is running out for our generation. The fact remains, however, that much is at stake and there is a critical need for a new outpouring of God's Spirit among His people. May the great Invigilator grant us time and favour and a visitation of His power and glory in our lives that we may ultimately hear His adjudication (for He also is the examiner) "Well done."

In assessing the need for a new visitation of the Spirit of God in His Church, my approach has been to look squarely at the fundamentals of the Christian faith and consider how and why they are lacking within today's Church and, more specifically, in my own life. As a member of the dominant "boomer" generation, I must share in the responsibility for the degree to which the Church has drifted from the narrow path that defines Biblical Christianity.

The prophet Haggai announces that the glory of the latter "*house*," the abode of God, is to be greater than the former (Haggai 2:9, NASB). My premise is that just as the prophet instructed the people of Israel to go to the mountains and bring down timber to rebuild the house of the Lord (Haggai 1:8), there are certain mountains of the Scriptures that we ought to revisit in order to repair the "latter house" in preparation for a renewal of the Lord's glorious presence in His Church, i.e., in our lives. In chapter one we set the stage and establish the need to begin the process of rebuilding the Lord's house. In chapter two we go to the "mountain of obedience" where Abraham said an unqualified "yes" to God. In chapter three we ascend with Moses up the "mountain of truth." Chapter four takes us to the "mountain of hope" where Moses was shown the Promised Land. In chapter five we go with Elijah to the "mountain of faith." Chapter six takes us to a strategic mountain, the "mountain of revelation" where Jesus was transformed in the sight of Peter, James, and John. In chapter seven it's Mount Calvary, the "mountain of sacrifice," the theological centre of the whole narrative, and in chapter eight we look at Mount Zion, the "mountain of the Lord's presence." We conclude in chapters nine and ten with a call to a commitment to prayer and an injunction to remain faithful to the Great Commission.

My intention therefore is to stir within the reader a passion to rediscover the fundamentals of Christian life and faith to the end that the Holy Spirit might fulfill the message of the prophet Haggai in our time. I believe He will do so as we ready our own lives to be indwelt by the fullness of His Spirit.

Acknowledgements

As I WORKED THROUGH THE VARIOUS TOPICS AND SOUGHT to integrate life experiences into the fabric of this book, my wife, Brenda, has been a faithful and reliable editor and critic. I have highly valued her input and encouragement along the way.

Appreciation also goes to Dr. John Moore, who seemed to capture the spiritual impact I have desired to achieve in its writing and willingly shared from his rich life experiences to both encourage me and affirm the "compass bearing."

Thank you also to my friend John Hull, president of EQUIP and former senior pastor of The Peoples Church, for consistently affirming me and for his kind endorsement of this work.

Finally, my heartfelt thanks to Charles Price, who, out of his very busy work schedule, took time to read the manuscript and provide constructive feedback. His value-added endorsement and willingness to write the foreword have been deeply appreciated.

Acknowledgements

ONE

Time to Rebuild

"Go up into the mountains and bring down timber and build the house, so that I may take pleasure in it and be honored," says the Lord.

(Haggai 1:8)

I THOUGHT THEN, AND I MAINTAIN TODAY, THAT RURAL Newfoundland is *the* place to grow up. For my own part, in a family of six siblings, two sisters and four brothers, there was no shortage of challenge and adventure—each season bringing new and previously untested opportunities of discovery. I remember playing soccer in a tiny clearing at the edge of a woodlot in the spring; enjoying long, hot (yes, in Newfoundland!) days of summer with unlimited swimming in the local pond, trout fishing (and catching lots!) with a bamboo rod; berry picking to one's heart's content and cutting firewood and creating huge bonfires in the fall; and unlimited sledding, skating, and winter hiking over the frozen hills in a quest to sight rabbits, moose, or any other creature of the forest—real or imagined. As I recall the sheer simplicity of those days, as much as I might long for them I know they can never be recaptured. Their value today is in the richness of the memories they hold and in the lessons they still teach.

The shout of "Timber!" commonly could be heard above the roar of the chainsaw on a cold but sunny winter's day. The dense forests of the nearby hills offered a ready supply of logs. I can still hear the crunch of horse's hoofs on the compacted snow as men of the village would make use of the frozen and snow-covered trails to haul the newly hewn logs—wood to fuel the stoves and provide warmth in the wood-frame dwellings. It was also not unusual for the resourceful Newfoundlander to haul timber from the hills to the sawmill. From the trees on the hills to the completion of a sturdy house, he would see the project of home construction through from start to finish. The acquisition of timber always had an intended purpose. Sometimes it simply meant a house was in need of extension or repair.

Lessons learned in those far away formative years now surpass the surface understanding I then had of how things got done. They, together with my grown-up (I trust!) spiritual insights, serve to enhance my appreciation of spiritual truths and enable me to make ready application to how we ought to address the issues facing the Church today.

Securing timber from the mountains is a directive forming a clear mandate, given to the people of God through the prophet Haggai—timber for the building and repair of the house of God. But construction cannot begin until the timber is found. The mandate comes to Haggai with a certain degree of urgency, as a correction of perspective is in order. The people are suffering frustration and loss as a direct result of neglect—of neglecting the state of disrepair found in the temple, the house of God.

> Now therefore, thus says the LORD of hosts: "Consider your ways! You have sown much, and bring in little; You eat, but do not have enough; You drink, but you are not filled with drink; You clothe yourselves, but no one is warm; And he who earns wages, Earns wages to put into a bag with holes." Thus says the LORD of hosts: "Consider your ways!" (Haggai 1:5–7 NKJV).

The issue in Haggai's day was not that the people had turned their backs on God as their ancestors had repeatedly done. It was that their priorities had shifted. They weren't guilty of bold rebellion—just of neglect. They contented themselves by saying that this was not the Lord's time for attention to be given to the temple. "This is what the LORD Almighty says: 'These people say, "The time has not yet come for the LORD's house to be built"'" (Haggai 1:2). Instead they focused on their personal needs and projects and gave secondary attention to the things of God. It's easy to do—and we're no different. Life presses in on us. There are family issues, work issues, social demands, car repairs, house repairs, and bills to pay. The list is endless, and, though we mean to

> The issue in Haggai's day was not that the people had turned their backs on God as their ancestors had repeatedly done. It was that their priorities had shifted.

be faithful, before we know it we become caught in never-ending cycles of obligation, just in order to survive. Or so it seems! As we take stock of the degree of loss—the spiritual health of God's people—in the Church in our time, could it be that it's time to hear the shout of "timber" as we go to the mountains and bring home the supplies necessary to strengthen and repair the house of God? It will take some soul-searching and discipline, but I believe the time is now.

The Need for Repair

Have you taken a look lately at the state of repair of the Lord's house? Is there disrepair? What are the indicators? When the structure begins to weaken, when there is obvious decay that impedes its readiness to protect from outside elements, when the cracks in the walls allow the light from the outside world to penetrate, when there is a disintegration from within— attention to repair is warranted.

This is not another book to condemn the practices and prejudices of the evangelical Church—to point out how terribly we have failed to fulfill the New Testament mandate to be salt and light. The print media offers no shortage of searing indictments against the Church in which you and I grew up. *Irrelevant, insular,* and *legalistic* are some of the common adjectives used to describe a twentieth-century Church that had lost its way. Such indictments have been trumpeted as new methodologies have been introduced to redefine and relaunch the Church in a renewed, more culturally relevant packaging. My purpose is not to join the bandwagon but to suggest that—in spite of such recent attempts to morph the Church into a kinder, gentler, more culturally aware institution—we continue to observe growing cracks and disintegration of our moral and spiritual fabric. Our state of disrepair can be traced to some key pillars. Before we explore the wisdom to be gleaned from a survey of certain strategic and prominent mountains from the narratives of Scripture, let's take an honest look at some of the cracks, some of the shabbiness to be observed as we take an evaluative look about.

And a look about, for the purpose of identifying the need for renewal, is all that's required. I think of our easygoing approach to discipleship, the lack of evidence of the spiritual disciplines in the lives of God's people, and the shallow treatment of the Word of God by pastors and teachers so as to make Christianity palatable and "relevant" to the culture. Perhaps more alarming (except that nothing is really alarming any more, which may in itself be a statement of our collective spiritual conscience) are the latest statistics regarding failed marriages within the evangelical Church and the weakening of the nuclear family. Add to that the research findings regarding the viewpoint of the emerging generation of "believers" on such previous non-negotiables as salvation through Christ alone, the eternal judgment of the lost, and the authority and infallibility of the Scriptures. While reflecting on these negative realities one day recently I came upon an item in *Virtual House News,* an on-line magazine sponsored by the Evangelical Fellowship of Canada. The magazine featured an interview with well-known apologist Josh McDowell. McDowell has established himself as a voice of integrity within the evangelical world, and his comments were no less than startling. Commenting on his recent findings regarding the current beliefs of evangelical youth, here's what he says:

> It's a crisis. Right now within twelve months of high school graduation 80 to 85 percent of our kids are walking away from the Church. If we keep doing what we're doing it will soon be 90 percent.

> According to Barna 65 percent of our churched kids either suspect or believe there is no way to tell which religion is true. In 1994 52 percent of evangelical Christian kids said, "There is no truth apart from myself." In 1999 that number jumped to 78 percent. Now it is a staggering 91 percent. Sixty-three percent of our kids say, "Jesus Christ is not the Son of God. He's *a* son of God." If you say there is no truth then you can't make the statement consistently that Jesus is the Son of God. Francis Schaeffer said, "Culture has become post-Christian." I believe now he would say it's become anti-Christian.[1]

How has it become possible for the Church to have undergone this degree of assimilation into the mainstream? How is it that we find it so accepting of the world view of popular culture? John the apostle clearly tells us what our approach to the worldly system, in which we are required to live, should be: *"Do not love the world or anything in the world. If anyone loves the world, the love of the Father is not in him"* (1 John 2:15).

How do we view the world? Do we see the world

around us as a system to emulate or as souls to be loved and rescued? When the Church has a healthy God-consciousness it reflects the heart of God for His world. Do we as the Church of today manifest a passion for the souls of the earth's peoples, or do we fail to be motivated to minister God's love to a spiritually dying world? Do our concerns for the broken and dispossessed of our world merely mirror the humanitarian concerns of society at large? Statistics show that as much as 96 percent of the North American Church's resources stay in North America! Surely that kind of measurement speaks to us about our heart of concern for the lost. Yes, there are large structural deficiencies in the Lord's house—enough to spur us to action if we would only take notice.

Defining "the Lord's House"

This critique of the state of the "house of God" has both individual and corporate reference. *"Do you not know that your body is a temple of the Holy Spirit, who is in you, whom you have received from God? You are not your own"* (1 Corinthians 6:19). You and I ought to tremble at the very thought that God in His greatness, His holiness, has cleansed us and designed us to be His dwelling place. You and I have become, through an incredible act of creative grace, the abode of His presence, the accommodation of His divine life, and the channel of His peace and redemptive love in the world. What a thought! I trust that the exercise we are embarking on will make a difference in our perspective. Let's believe that as we consider the potential need for repair of God's dwelling place—the Church of today—

you and I will allow the Word of God to be a mirror that convicts us of the state of our personal lives.

A rare yet interesting experience for me as a young boy was, on a rainy day, to secure the permission of my parents to take a bright flashlight and climb into the attic of our outport home. (*Outport* is the term for a Newfoundland fishing village.) The bright light would penetrate the darkness of the attic and show clearly the defects of the wood. It would show the layers of dust and would readily reveal where water might be seeping through, threatening the integrity of the roof boards. In Stephen's address to the Sanhedrin in Acts chapter seven he presents the truth about the revolutionary teaching of the New Testament: *"The Most High does not live in houses made by men"* (Acts 7:48). You and I are now the dwelling place of God. We must let the light of the Spirit of truth illumine the inner condition of our lives and be ready to apply corrective action.

> You and I have become, through an incredible act of creative grace, the abode of His presence, the accommodation of His divine life, and the channel of His peace and redemptive love in the world.

We need also to consider ourselves as responsible members of the corporate structure—as living stones within the local and global spiritual house. Read carefully what the apostle Peter has to say on this subject:

> *You also, like living stones,* **are being built into a spiritual house to be a holy priesthood,** *offering spiritual sacrifices acceptable to God through Jesus Christ. For in Scripture it says: "See, I lay a stone in*

Zion, a chosen and precious cornerstone, and the one who trusts in him will never be put to shame." Now to you who believe, this stone is precious. But to those who do not believe, "The stone the builders rejected has become the capstone," and, "A stone that causes men to stumble and a rock that makes them fall." They stumble because they disobey the message—which is also what they were destined for. But you are a chosen people, a royal priesthood, a holy nation, a people belonging to God, that you may declare the praises of him who called you out of darkness into his wonderful light. Once you were not a people, but now you are the people of God; once you had not received mercy, but now you have received mercy. Dear friends, I urge you, as aliens and strangers in the world, to abstain from sinful desires, which war against your soul (1 Peter 2:5–11, emphasis added).

Peter clearly identifies us as being built together in a building whose foundation is Christ. We are linked with Him, set apart for His glory, designed to declare His praises, to manifest His goodness in a world of darkness. Is it possible that we have a tendency to take too lightly our distinct identity and role? *"Chosen," "royal," "holy"*—these are the adjectives that describe who we are! Because Christ has positionally granted us this distinction, ought we not to be concerned about whether our attitudes and actions—the state of the house—conform to His character and the values of His Word?

There's Timber in Those Mountains

This is what the LORD Almighty says: "Give careful thought to your ways. Go up into the mountains and bring down timber and build the house, so that I may take pleasure in it and be honored," says the LORD (Haggai 1:7,8).

As in all prophetic Scripture, the message of Haggai is spoken with directness and with a certain urgency. Repeatedly we hear *"Consider your ways."* In verse 8, *"Give careful thought to your ways"* precedes the directive to go and secure the timber. If the prophet were to speak directly to us today, I believe he would open his message with the same insistence. I know that, for my own part, I've been taken up with the important matters of life and church and, frankly, have little time for reflection and personal stock-taking. It's time for us to take a look at ourselves—to consider our ways and come face to face with a renewed concern about the condition of the house that God by His Spirit has chosen as His dwelling place! This, I believe, is what forms the single greatest impediment to the out-pouring of God's Spirit today. He is concerned about the condition of His house, and the ones who have been given responsibility for the care and upkeep of that house are you and I!

Realizing the need then for revision and repair of "the Lord's house," let us explore the value and the necessity of the "timbers" we might find on various strategic mountains of the Bible. I dare you to take a series of trips to the mountains of the Scriptures with me and examine the "timbers" that need to be harvested if the house of the Lord is to receive the attention and repair that is currently needed. Here are the mountains and the particular timbers we encounter as we explore each scene.

MOUNTAIN	TIMBER
Mt. Moriah	Obedience
Mt. Horeb (Sinai)	Truth
Mt. Pisgah	Hope
Mt. Carmel	Faith
Mt. of Transfiguration	Revelation
Mt. Calvary	Sacrifice
Mt. Zion	Presence
Mountain in Galilee	Commission

The timbers that these mountains provide, if harvested and used to rebuild the structure, have the potential to strengthen and refurbish the true Church of Jesus Christ. They together have the potential to make us into the dynamic, living house that God initially designed us to be, a place for His glory to dwell! Each mountain experience affords us the opportunity to rediscover the ancient paths—the truths that form the primary conditions for the presence and the activity of God in the lives of His people. As I ponder the need for the Church of today to revisit some of the qualities that define—or ought to define—us as the people of God, I'm all too aware of the need for renewal in my own life. I have no moral authority to point the finger at any individual or any institution for failing to apply the fundamentals of Biblical truth to prepare a place for the glory of the Lord to be seen. I do know that I have seen His greatest works, and experienced Him most fully, as I've walked up some of those mountains with Him. Somewhere, deep down inside of me, is a longing to have my soul renewed:

1) as I experience new levels of obedience
2) as I allow His truth to transform me
3) as I see His hope restored within me
4) as I maintain a strong position of faith
5) as I catch a fresh vision of the glorified Christ
6) as I explore the wonder of Calvary's love
7) as I desire to daily experience "the God who is present"
8) as I pray and allow His Spirit to work in me.

Let's go to the mountains! Let's harvest those essential timbers to prepare the house for a new visitation of the Lord of the Church!

As we begin the journey to those strategic mountains of the Word of God, let's open our minds and hearts and ask the Lord to bring Spirit-led awareness of what is lacking and what needs repair in our lives personally. Would you begin by praying the following prayer with me?

Dear Lord, how evident it is that Your house is seriously in need of repair! I confess before You that I need to rediscover and to reapply the Biblical dynamics of obedience, truth, hope, faith, revelation, and sacrifice so that I might be a witness of the glorious presence of the Lord in His house.

Forgive me for allowing the enemy to blind my eyes to spiritual reality. Forgive me for bringing reproach to You by placing You, through my actions and my inaction, in a secondary position. Forgive me for my selfish pursuits and for failing to value my life as the dwelling place of Christ. I desire to be reawakened to the urgency of the need for a fresh visitation of Your presence and power in us, Your Church.

I pray that You would restore to me a passionate desire to see Christ honoured and His people filled with knowledge and power. I pray this in order that we might demonstrate to the world the wonder, the beauty, the mercy, and the justice of a holy God.

Amen.

Mount Moriah:
The Mountain of Obedience

"Take your son, your only son, Isaac, whom you love, and go to the region of Moriah. Sacrifice him there as a burnt offering on one of the mountains I will tell you about"

(Genesis 22:2).

GROWING UP IN A PREACHER'S HOME HAD ITS PERKS—like at Christmastime when everyone in our little church community seemed to want to bring presents to the parsonage. Colouring books, paint-by-number sets, mittens, storybooks, and dinky cars would be among the treasures concealed by bright Christmas wrapping and placed under the tree until Christmas morning. You may have heard it said that Newfoundlanders are the kindest people on the face of the earth. It's true.

Being a member of the preacher's family also gave us some measure of prominence in the community, which sometimes worked to our advantage, like when teams were being "picked" on the school playground or fishing partners were being chosen. But growing up in a preacher's home also had its drawbacks. My dad would often speak fondly of "my boys"—in public!

When you're seven, eight, or nine, it's improper to crawl under the pew while a service is in progress. You get the picture! So you sit and die many deaths as your dad tells the world what an especially gifted kid you are. *Mortified* is a term that comes close to describing the horror. But the upside to my dad's expressions of fondness was for me the security of knowing that he would lay down his life for any one of us.

> My love for my sons enables me to grasp something of the deep, deep pain in the heart of Abraham as he approached the summit of Mt. Moriah.

I never fully understood my dad's love for us until I had grown and had my own sons. Early in our marriage the Lord blessed Brenda and me with Kent, our first-born, followed just under three years later with our second, Brad. They have drastically different personalities, but each is uniquely special to me. Though they themselves are now adults, Kent's and Brad's hurts are my hurts; their joys, my joys. I can't conceive of my world without them. I consider it my duty and privilege to pray daily for the Lord's will to be accomplished through them. My love for my sons enables me to grasp something of the deep, deep pain in the heart of Abraham as he approached the summit of Mt. Moriah, his son Isaac dutifully carrying the pile of wood for the burnt offering. The emotional pain could not have been more excruciating.

Trust in his dad would have by now grown strong in the boy, Isaac. He had witnessed time and again Abraham's faithfulness as he dutifully and regularly presented offerings to God. Isaac was not unfamiliar with the process—the building of the stone altar, the preparation of the fire, the laying on of the wood until the fire was burning vigorously. The Genesis 22 account tells us that it wasn't long before it struck him that there was a missing item—the lamb for the burnt offering. So he asked the question (Genesis 22:7). It had to strike Abraham like a dagger as he realized that he was getting closer to the moment. Sooner or later Abraham would have to face the inevitable. He would have to do the unthinkable—tie his son up and lay him on the altar.

The record of Scripture attests that *"he did not waver at the promise of God through unbelief"* (Romans 4:20 NKJV). Something tells me I might have wavered were I in Abraham's sandals that day. But then, Abraham's obedience was born out of an understanding that God requires total and absolute trust from His children. To disobey God is to take back the helm, thereby suggesting that God does not have my best interests at heart. My walk with God breaks down if He doesn't have my complete trust. And so I must ask myself again, "Is the plank of obedience firmly in place in the temple?"

"Something to do with Isaac"

I sometimes wonder if position and comfort are keeping me from experiencing the level of surrender that I once knew. As I reflect on the dramatic ways the Lord confirmed His Word and His call on my own life at certain times in my past, I grow hungry for such intimacy and such simple trust again.

It was in 1988 that the Lord told my wife, Brenda, and me to venture into an area that neither of us felt equipped to take on—namely, to begin an inner-city ministry in St. John's, Newfoundland. Evangelical churches, though at one time scattered over the downtown area, had virtually all moved to the higher levels of the city. The Lord clearly gave us a burden to plant a church in the heart of downtown and to begin to preach the message of salvation amidst the diverse and challenging downtown culture.

We were not long into the implementation of this vision when it became very clear that we would have to "downsize"—to readjust our lifestyle. This meant selling our relatively nice home in the east end of St. John's. It was during the early stages of this "adventure" that a rather unusual thing happened to me as one evening I was preparing a "For Sale" sign to place on the front lawn. My heart was heavy over the knowledge that this house represented some material security for Brenda's, the boys', and my future. As I talked to the Lord about the inner conflict I was experiencing, He said to me—not audibly, but definitely—"This for you is like offering up Isaac." This was a profound moment, but I have to say that it brought little comfort to me. There were aspects of that whole journey that were dark and painful. How could I deprive my sons of the opportunities that our (mine and Brenda's) professions could provide? How would I deal with our families' failure to understand? What would it do to my reputation of being a steady guy with a well-balanced approach to Christian living? What if I hadn't really heard from God in this? Yes, there were some pretty severe internal battles I had to fight—battles arising from my own feelings of pride, insecurity, and, at times, unbelief. Yet, the direction had been set and we had embarked on a journey of faith, attempting to walk in simple obedience to His voice.

I shared the particular "Isaac" experience with no one. A short time later on a Sunday, a small group had gathered for a service in what was now our little church in downtown St. John's. Just prior to the start of the service a young man approached me and offered me an envelope. Remarkably, the envelope contained a cheque that would cover most of our personal expenses for that month. What was more remarkable though was the statement he made as he handed me the envelope: "Pastor Reg, I feel that God has directed me to give you this—and I don't know what this means but He seemed to say to me that it has something to do with Isaac." No, not an audible voice from heaven, but a strong and clear affirmation that the Lord was pleased with my act of obedience! Reflecting on that special time of hearing the voice of the Lord (and obeying), I ask myself, ought not such communion and confirmation be normative for the Church in which His presence dwells? Yet for me such intimacy with Him seems all too remote today.

Author John Phillips points out that *Moriah* means "foreseen of Jehovah."[2] The words of Ephesians 2:10 come to mind: *"For we are God's workmanship, created in Christ Jesus to do good works, which God prepared in advance for us to do."* God has foreordained the path that we should walk and has foreseen and prepared the specific acts of service we are to perform. It makes sense then that we walk in communion with Him and obediently carry out the work which He, the Master

Designer, has given us to do. For this to be accomplished there is a need for the "plank of obedience" to be restored to His house.

Trust and Obey

As I ponder the place of simple obedience my mind settles on another snapshot from my childhood. With my mom pounding out the melody on the piano, the service drew to a close with a robust rendition of "Trust and Obey." I, at age eight, could sing all of the words from all of the stanzas by heart: "When we walk with the Lord in the light of His Word, what a glory He sheds on our way...Not a shadow can rise, not a cloud in the skies...But we never can prove the delights of His love until all on the altar we lay..." and finally the chorus: "Trust and obey, for there's no other way to be happy in Jesus, but to trust and obey." No mezzo sounds there! What we got was an expression of unrefined chorus—loud and hearty singing from happy saints, old and young, who seemed to have a genuine sense that what they were singing was truth—objective truth, yes, because they would never question the authority and veracity of Scripture. For many of them, the truth was also refreshingly subjective, as alive and up-to-date testimonies had borne witness in the service. They gave reports of the faithfulness of God as they entrusted their families, their vocations (in most cases fishing), and their struggles to Him.

My parents would continue to lead the enthusiastic round of song, singing the last verse over a second time. In the midst of this snapshot of basic Christian experience, expressed in vigorous song, Dad and Mom too had a story to tell. They had known what it was to venture out in what they felt was a step of obedience to preach the gospel of Christ. For them there had been no guarantee of income or of supportive resources of any kind. They understood the importance of a Mt. Moriah walk of obedience. With that knowledge as a backdrop, engrained in the world view of our family was the fact that Christ was all and in all, and the expectation was that we would be available to go wherever God would lead us. My mom, in particular, worked that conflict through with some anguish as she dedicated her life to prayer for her family, even long after we had left home.

A pertinent question arises but is not one that is easy to confront. John Phillips in *The View from Mount Calvary* writes concerning Abraham's inner conflict:

> Let us walk awhile with Abraham as he set out with Isaac, with an ass, and with a couple of men. Abraham himself chopped the wood for the fire. Mental pictures of the place would loom up in his mind. He would see, perhaps, a towering crag, its face blasted by lightning and gouged into fearful shapes by tempest, earthquake and storm. At other times, maybe, he saw a tortured, twisting path leading down into a gorge in the mountain and ending near some dark cave.[2]

How the physical environment of that mountain must have seemed austere and unwelcoming to him! We have a tendency to cast Bible heroes like Abraham in a superhuman light. The reality was that he dealt with incredible internal conflict. From the Genesis 22 account we get a sense of the depth of emotional conflict Abraham must have endured. Let's walk with him as he undertakes a three day's journey, as he has his men wait while he and Isaac proceed up the mountain, as he places the burden of the wood on Isaac's back, and as he attempts to maintain his composure when they approach the designated place for the sacrifice.

> On the third day Abraham looked up and saw the place in the distance. He said to his servants, "Stay here with the donkey while I and the boy go over there. We will worship and then we will come back to you." Abraham took the wood for the burnt offering and placed it on his son Isaac, and he himself carried the fire and the knife. As the two of them went on together, Isaac spoke up and said to his father Abraham, "Father?" "Yes, my son?" Abraham replied. "The fire and wood are here," Isaac said, "but where is the lamb for the burnt offering?" Abraham answered, "God himself will provide the lamb for the burnt offering, my son." And the two of them went on together (Genesis 22:4–8).

Then he began to build the altar, the altar on which he would slay his son. All this added up to a drawn out, agonizing trial for him. At the moment Abraham lifted the knife to perform the execution of his own son, it seems to me that he would have reached a point of total brokenness. Obedience had broken him and brought him to a place of total dependence on God. That's where obedience normally takes the believer!

Here's the question that comes to us today: *Are we*

willing to release our sons, our daughters, into the hands of God? Are we willing to let them go to the hostile environments of the "majority world" for the sake of fulfilling His will—His command? A Church that is alive with a realization of the glory of God is a Church that has a vital global consciousness and is highly motivated towards acts of obedience. A study in the history of revivals will show that renewal in the Church has always resulted in many young men and women traveling across oceans and continents to bring the light of the gospel to remote regions of the earth. The twentieth-century outpouring among the hundreds of thousands of believers in South Korea has resulted in thousands of Koreans taking the gospel to many areas of the world, including the "creative access" regions of the 10–40 window. Where is the passion for souls that was the driving force behind the world missions movement of the early twentieth century? A Church that walks in obedience is a Church that is dedicated to world evangelization.

> But on a practical level—down where you and I live—obedience does not necessarily require acts of daring and gallantry. It boils down to the simple choices we make in our daily living.

But on a practical level—down where you and I live—obedience does not necessarily require acts of daring and gallantry. It boils down to the simple choices we make in our daily living. The choice to spend time in meditation instead of viewing our favourite TV program; the choice of devoting daily time to the oft neglected discipline of prayer; the choice of taking time to spend a few moments assisting a neighbour in need or sharing food with the hungry of our city. You could extend my list to include many other examples to help characterize what obedient service looks like—things we ought to do but don't.

Fundamentally, it's self-denial, is it not? What we observe of Abraham on Mt. Moriah is a supreme act of self-denial. Self-denial is (or ought to be) at the very root of our Christian walk. *"If anyone would come after me, he must deny himself and take up his cross daily and follow me"* (Luke 9:23). In our "me-centred" world the notion of self-denial runs counter to popular thought and wisdom. Obedience never comes easy. There is always some risk, some cost, touching some area of our lives where pain and discomfort are inevitable. Yet it forms the very essence of what the Lord requires of us. But how do I get from my current state of mediocrity to again see the Lord at work in me?

There is something that the intense drama of the story tends to eclipse. It can be found in the words of Abraham as he answers his inquisitive son: *"God himself will provide the lamb"* (Genesis 22:8). Abraham's trust, and therefore his obedience, came out of relationship. That's why the Scriptures record that he did not waver at God's promises through unbelief (Romans 4:20). He knew God in a way that mandated obedience even when the potential cost was unthinkable.

Henry Blackaby highlights the central importance of relationship in the Abraham story:

> Abraham knew the voice of God and therefore knew when God was speaking. Do you clearly, unmistakably know the voice of God when He is speaking to

you? If not, you are in trouble at the heart of your relationship with God. I am not talking about hearing an audible voice but rather learning to hear the voice of God through the Scriptures. How can you obey Him if you never know when He is speaking? If obedience to His voice was the key to Abraham's relationship with God...then obedience to God's voice is crucial to our relationship with God![3]

This, I confess, is my greatest need as I survey the landscape of my own walk—busy with doing the Lord's work while failing to foster a relationship with Him. If you find yourself where I am, if the Church in general is in the same boat, no wonder the plank of obedience needs strengthening! Would you take a moment to consider the need to repair the plank of obedience in your life and in the Church and pray the following prayer with me?

Dear Lord, I confess that I, through selfishness and neglect, have failed to give first importance to the need of growing my relationship with You. I have walked in disobedience, resulting in wrong choices in the small decisions of life, so that You've been unable to entrust the more weighty decisions to me. I have dishonoured You, my Lord, by relegating You as an "add-on" to my list of obligations. In sincerity of heart, I repent.

Let my relationship with You become like that of Abraham, so that I'm ready to entrust all that I am and have to You. Let me be willing to respond to Your voice even when it costs dearly.

Let my life become again a vessel of worship—an expression of full surrender. Let obedience be restored to my life in particular, and to Your "house" in general, to make way for a fresh impartation of Your glory.

Amen.

THREE

Mount Sinai:
The Mountain of Truth

When the LORD finished speaking to Moses on Mount Sinai, he gave him the two tablets of the Testimony, the tablets of stone inscribed by the finger of God

(Exodus 31:18).

I WAS NOT AWARE GROWING UP (AT LEAST NOT AS AWARE AS I am today) of just how legalistic my cultural religious tradition had become. Ladies wearing pants or makeup or seamless nylons (a term altogether unfamiliar to today's thirty-somethings and younger) was simply forbidden! I heard stories of men shaving on Saturday night in order to avoid having to shave on Sunday, the Sabbath. "Do's and don'ts" abounded—not unlike the myriads of regulations that had evolved in Jewish religious tradition in Jesus' day, prompting sharp rebuke from the Master on more than one occasion. My parents, nevertheless, had influenced my thinking so that I understood the supreme power of God's grace. At the same time they instilled in me a healthy fear of the Lord. The Ten Commandments were just that—the Ten Commandments, not the Ten Suggestions. At no time did I feel I had the liberty to interpret the commandments to suit myself. The Decalogue was viewed as God's word to us, not as a list of debatable moral points to be modified and adapted according to situational realities.

Not that the commandments are the full embodiment of Biblical truth, but our attitude towards them, I believe, is a reflection of how we value and revere the entirety of Scripture. The importance of the Word of God—the veracity of the Scriptures and their incomparable value to me as a guide and a resource governing every aspect of faith and life—could not have been emphasized more fully than they were during my growing up years. The psalmist David leaves us no doubt concerning the value and the place of the Word of God in our lives.

> The Decalogue was viewed as God's word to us, not as a list of debatable moral points to be modified and adapted according to situational realities.

> *The law of the LORD is perfect, reviving the soul. The statutes of the LORD are trustworthy, making wise the simple. The precepts of the LORD are right, giving joy to the heart. The commands of the LORD are radiant, giving light to the eyes. The fear of the LORD is pure, enduring forever. The ordinances of the LORD are sure and altogether righteous. They are more precious than gold, than much pure gold; they are sweeter than honey, than honey from the comb. By them is your servant warned; in keeping them there is great reward* (Psalm 19:7–11).

So the Word of God held a place of prominence and reverence in my upbringing. Through daily family devotions, Scripture memorization, and the importance consistently ascribed to the Bible's teachings, we were led to have the highest regard for the truth of God's Word. To defy or attempt to reinterpret Scripture to suit our private viewpoints or personal preferences was unthinkable.

Moses Receives God's Changeless Truth

I've always found Moses' encounter with God on Mt. Sinai an awesome and intriguing scene. It is one of those unusual times in Scripture when we observe God interacting directly with man. Thunder, fire, smoke, the quaking of the mountain, the voice of God, the glory of God—all convey an awesomeness, a transcendence, that speaks to me of ultimate authority and supreme power. It is in this context that the law is presented. Here's the Exodus record:

> "I am the LORD your God, who brought you out of Egypt, out of the land of slavery."
> "You shall have no other gods before me."
> "You shall not make for yourself an idol in the form of anything in heaven above or on the earth beneath or in the waters below. You shall not bow down to them or worship them; for I, the LORD your God, am a jealous God, punishing the children for the sin of the fathers to the third and fourth generation of those who hate me, but showing love to a thousand generations of those who love me and keep my commandments."
> "You shall not misuse the name of the LORD your

God, for the Lord will not hold anyone guiltless who misuses his name."

"Remember the Sabbath day by keeping it holy. Six days you shall labor and do all your work, but the seventh day is a Sabbath to the LORD your God. On it you shall not do any work, neither you, nor your son or daughter, nor your manservant or maidservant, nor your animals, nor the alien within your gates. For in six days the LORD made the heavens and the earth, the sea, and all that is in them, but he rested on the seventh day. Therefore the LORD blessed the Sabbath day and made it holy."

"Honor your father and your mother, so that you may live long in the land the LORD your God is giving you."

"You shall not murder."

"You shall not commit adultery."

"You shall not steal."

"You shall not give false testimony against your neighbor."

"You shall not covet your neighbor's house. You shall not covet your neighbor's wife, or his manservant or maidservant, his ox or donkey, or anything that belongs to your neighbor."

When the people saw the thunder and lightning and heard the trumpet and saw the mountain in smoke, they trembled with fear. They stayed at a distance and said to Moses, "Speak to us yourself and we will listen. But do not have God speak to us or we will die" (Exodus 20:2–19).

And I say, "How dare I relegate its importance to a "take it or leave it" position?" In actuality, Jesus affirms the Mosaic law without qualification: *I tell you the truth, until heaven and earth disappear, not the smallest letter, not the least stroke of a pen, will by any means disappear from the Law until everything is accomplished*" (Matthew 5:18). The conflict becomes personal and deflating, though, when we read Jesus' commentary:

> *"You have heard that it was said to the people long ago, 'Do not murder, and anyone who murders will be subject to judgment.' But I tell you that anyone who is angry with his brother will be subject to judgment. Again, anyone who says to his brother, 'Raca,' is answerable to the Sanhedrin. But anyone who says, 'You fool!' will be in danger of the fire of hell*" (Matthew 5:21,22).

Similarly, *"You have heard that it was said, 'Do not commit adultery.' But I tell you that anyone who looks at a woman lustfully has already committed adultery with her in his heart*" (Matthew 5:26,27). So has God changed His mind on such issues as adultery, fornication, the Sabbath, covetousness, and the like? If anything, Jesus raised the standard even higher! When we take an honest look at these "unrealistic" expectations we soon realize that neither you nor I can live up to them. We miss the mark time and again.

Then how can we even begin to address the issues of godlessness and seeming disregard for the righteous standards of a holy God? Is it just me, or has the Church in general defaulted to a defeatist position on the whole question of the commandments? Have we caved to the enemy and taken the stance that since we are unable to meet the requirements, we might as well excuse ourselves from making any attempt? It seems to me that we're saying, "We're bound to fail, so why bother?" "If you can't beat 'em, join 'em." On the matter of divorce alone some statistics suggest that the percentage of failed marriages within the evangelical Church is as great as that within the secular world. This simply means that, according to the Biblical definition of adultery, God's law is being broken at an alarming rate within the Church. Ron Sider in *The Scandal of the Evangelical Conscience* calls the Church on its immoral conduct:

> Born-again Christians justify and engage in sexual promiscuity (both premarital sex and adultery) at astonishing rates. Racism and perhaps physical abuse of wives seem to be worse in evangelical circles than elsewhere. This is scandalous behavior for people who claim to be born again by the Holy Spirit and to enjoy the very presence of the risen Lord in their lives.[4]

How does one begin to address a situation that has devolved to the extent that Sider cites? I must somehow get beyond the shock of such realities and realize that the starting point must be my own heart. More on that later.

Never on Sunday

Then, there's the Sabbath. Clearly the "Sabbath" commandment was given, like all the other commandments, to be observed. When one is eight, nine, or ten years old, one holds a passion for everything "out-doors." Skating on the frozen pond, trout fishing through a hole in the ice, sleighing on a steep and slip-pery hill, and jumping from one broken piece of ice to another along the shoreline (known locally as "copying pans") were among the activities that I revelled in as a child. My parents were inclined to allow us to drink in these adventures and live life to the fullest. Apart from the requirement of doing some domestic chores, we were essentially given a blank cheque to lap up these experiences and enjoy, in the process, the strong social ties we forged with other kids in the community. These experiences were what defined our lives growing up—carefree and full of adventure. We just knew, and our friends knew, we couldn't do them on a Sunday! Sunday was "the Lord's day," and from our earliest days we understood that the Lord's day was set apart for worship and quiet.

As I opened this chapter I referred in negative tones to the legalism that seemed at times in our religious tra-dition to define Christianity as a rule-oriented religion. In retrospect I see that, with the right perspective, such observances instilled a fear of the Lord—a deep respect for His righteous ways. My theological insights have matured since those days. I understand the need to not be bound by specific days. Paul gives a word of clarity on this issue in his letter to the Colossians:

Therefore do not let anyone judge you by what you eat or drink, or with regard to a religious festival, a New Moon celebration or a Sabbath day. These are a shadow of the things that were to come; the reality, however, is found in Christ (Colossians 2:16,17).

So it seems that the question of which day we observe as our Sabbath is not as critical as some seem to think. Nor do I wish to diminish the value of celebrating the first day of the week as the Lord's day. What I do ask myself time and again is this: "Am I neglecting to understand and walk in the truth concerning the Sabbath? Why does faithlessness keep me from enjoying the great liberty that Christ has provided? Why do I fail to revel in the grace, the goodness, the salvation, and the rest of the Lord?" Mark Buchanan has recently written *The Rest of God: Restoring Your Soul By Restoring the Sabbath,* in which he suggests that the Church of today has allowed itself to be overcome by life's overload, and the Sabbath is out the window.

> But what about Sabbath? Sabbath was made for man. It was something God prepared long ago, inscribed into the very order of creation: a day when all the other days loosed their grip. They were forced to. It's the day God intended to fuss over us, not we over it. It was designed to protect us, pay tribute to us, coddle us, in all our created frailty and God-imprinted beauty and hard-won liberty in our status as men and women whom God made in his own image and freed by his own hand and own blood.[5]

So when we bemoan the fact that Sunday has become "like any other day," what ought to concern us most is not that the observance of a particular day is lost on today's younger generation but that it represents a loss of knowledge or regard for the truth of God's Word. Concerning this, and all the other commandments, Charles Price, senior pastor of The Peoples

Church in Toronto, gives a teaching highlighting that due to the power of the indwelling Christ, who takes up residence in each believer, the commandments of the Old Testament become promises in the New. Our victory over evil and our walking in righteousness are enabled by the supernatural power of the indwelling Christ. What a liberating thought!

But you ask—and the question is fair—"Why is the Church's performance in the area of observing God's holy law so abysmal, so similar to the world?" Here's how I see it. The concept of the life of Christ within us presumes a vital relationship with God. That's the crux of the matter, and that's where we fall down.

> Our victory over evil and our walking in righteousness are enabled by the supernatural power of the indwelling Christ. What a liberating thought!

Jesus affirms in Matthew 22:37,38 what the first and greatest commandment is: "'*Love the Lord your God with all your heart and with all your soul and with all your mind.' This is the first and greatest commandment.*" Our failure to walk according to God's truth is wrapped up in this. We have failed to love the One who is Himself the Truth. We fail to love Him with our hearts (our innermost selves), refusing to reflect on His amazing love for us. We fail to live in the Sabbath rest He has provided—in the place of communion and peace. We fail to love Him with our souls (the centre of our wills), making daily choices that ignore Him. We fail to love Him with our minds, refusing to take the time to be caught up in the wonder of His loftiness, His transcendence, His amazing creative power and wisdom. That is why our record is so poor. That's why His glory, the testimony of His presence, is scarcely seen in the Church today. We are missing the mark when it comes to the application of Biblical truth, because we don't have a love relationship with the "Word made flesh."

John the apostle addresses the subject in very plain language:

> We know that we have come to know him if we obey his commands. The man who says, "I know him," but does not do what he commands is a liar, and the truth is not in him. But if anyone obeys his word, God's love is truly made complete in him. This is how we know we are in him: Whoever claims to live in him must walk as Jesus did (1 John 2:3–6).

As I see it, there's not much need to exegete this passage, except perhaps to look carefully at the word *know.* The Greek word is *ginosko,* and it implies intimacy. There is a strong correlation between our love for the Lord and our appreciation of His truth. The one who lacks a living relationship with Christ is not normally inclined to carry a holy regard for the truth of the Word in his or her life. Those who espouse legalistic attempts to observe the Scriptures strictly as a discipline are often able to put forward a pious facade, yet they fail miserably in areas of personal pride and genuine love for others. Jesus very clearly makes the link between loving God and upholding His Word in John 14:21: "*Whoever has my commands and obeys them, he is the one who loves me. He who loves me will be loved by my Father, and I too will love him and show myself to him.*"

Not Mt. Horeb but Mt. Zion

Moses, after he had witnessed the awesomeness of the presence of God, understood how totally essential it was to have His presence remain with the people as they moved towards the Promised Land. He expressed his position clearly to the Lord in this simple but profound petition: *"If your Presence does not go with us, do not send us up from here"* (Exodus 33:15). Then he makes the request that ought to be the impassioned plea of the Church today—*"Show me your glory"* (Exodus 33:18).

The Lord's response to Moses is one that ought to greatly encourage our hearts. Here's the exchange:

> *And the LORD said to Moses, "I will do the very thing you have asked, because I am pleased with you and I know you by name." Then Moses said, "Now show me your glory." And the LORD said, "I will cause all my goodness to pass in front of you, and I will proclaim my name, the LORD, in your presence"* (Exodus 33:17–19).

God is not averse to displaying His presence to and among His people, and He let Moses know that his request was not out of line. He delights to manifest His character, His strength, and His majesty to His people, but—and here's the catch—the conditions have to be right.

> *Then the LORD said, "There is a place near me where you may stand on a rock. When my glory passes by, I will put you in a cleft in the rock and cover you with my hand until I have passed by"* (Exodus 33:21,22).

The symbolism is powerful and transferable into your experience and mine. If we are to see the glory as Moses did, we do so from the foundation, Jesus Christ, the Rock on which the Church is built. We will look at this again in chapter 8.

> If we are to see the glory as Moses did, we do so from the foundation, Jesus Christ, the Rock on which the Church is built.

The writer to the Hebrews makes a direct reference to the people of God at Mt. Sinai and contrasts that occurrence with the incredible reality of New Testament experience:

You have not come to a mountain that can be touched and that is burning with fire; to darkness, gloom and storm; to a trumpet blast or to such a voice speaking words that those who heard it begged that no further word be spoken to them, because they could not bear what was commanded: "If even an animal touches the mountain, it must be stoned." The sight was so terrifying that Moses said, "I am trembling with fear." But you have come to Mount Zion, to the heavenly Jerusalem, the city of the living God. You have come to thousands upon thousands of angels in joyful assembly, to the church of the first-born, whose names are written in heaven. You have come to God, the judge of all men, to the spirits of righteous men made perfect, to Jesus the mediator of a new covenant (Hebrews 12:18–24).

The fact that we have access to the same overwhelming presence of God through the new and living Way, *"Jesus the mediator of a new covenant,"* gives the

New Testament believer great advantage over the people of Moses' day. The covering of the blood of Christ makes all the difference. Through Him we may enter the very throne room of God (Hebrews 4:16). Yet, lest we too quickly breathe a sigh of relief and haste towards the conclusion that for us there is no cause for concern, the writer goes on to say something quite sobering. *"Therefore, since we are receiving a kingdom that cannot be shaken, let us be thankful, and so worship God acceptably with reverence and awe, for our 'God is a consuming fire'"* (Hebrews 12:28,29). God hasn't changed. His presence, though we are given ready access through the shed blood of Christ, ought to still evoke a holy fear (a reverence—a profound respect) in the hearts of His people.

Our careless attitude towards the commandments, I'm afraid, is a reflection of our approach to the Word of God generally. Today's Christian teachers and preachers by and large tend to steer away from the hard teachings of the Bible and towards the "feel good" stories of blessing and grace. Balanced teaching on the nature of God—His perfect justice as well as His perfect love—is not easily found. For many it's not an easy choice. We all seek acceptance and approval. It's important to the congregational leader to have a "respectable" approval rating within his audience. Unfortunately there are many today who value the approval of the people above the mandate they

> His presence, though we are given ready access through the shed blood of Christ, ought to still evoke a holy fear (a reverence—a profound respect) in the hearts of His people.

have been given through the calling of God on their lives. I am thankful for those men and women who resist the temptation to satisfy their audience through soft-pedalling but are instead willing to risk popularity and acceptance by delivering the whole truth. Unfortunately, my fear is that such faithful teachers are more the exception than the rule.

Revivalist Leonard Ravenhill was searing in much of his writings on the state of the mid-twentieth-century Church. In 1959 he wrote the following:

> One of these days some simple soul will pick up the Book of God, read it, and believe it. Then the rest of us will be embarrassed. We have adopted the convenient theory that the Bible is a Book to be explained, whereas first and foremost it is a Book to be believed (and after that to be obeyed). The fact beats ceaselessly in my brain these days that there is a world of difference between knowing the Word of God and knowing the God of the Word...Perhaps God never had such a set of unbelieving believers as this present crop of Christians.[6]

I'm reminded of the prophet Amos as he spoke prophetically of the day when there would be "*a famine of hearing the words of the LORD*" (Amos 8:11). Can this be true of our day? The Church of today would be well served if we were to go again to the "mountain of truth" and begin to value God's Word as we ought.

Would you take a moment with me and reflect on the need for reconsecration of our hearts before the Lord and pray the following?

Dear Lord, I have been guilty of ignoring the importance of the place Your living Word must have in my life. My estrangement from You has caused me to undermine Your holy law. May my love for Your Son Jesus Christ deepen, and may I walk in holiness through the power of His indwelling presence. I ask You to take me back again to the mountain of truth.

Let Your Church regain a deep respect for the authority of Your Word. Forgive us for profaning Your holy law by allowing its effect to erode so that we are barely distinguishable from the unregenerate world around us. Restore the plank of truth to Your house again in preparation for a new display of Your glory.

And for your servants whom You've called to proclaim Your Word, we pray for steel-like courage to declare the whole truth regardless of the feedback. Raise up Spirit-empowered ministers of truth who will preach the gospel of the Kingdom without compromise. May Your Church together manifest the distinctiveness from the world that Your Word so clearly requires. May the result be a new visitation of Your Spirit among Your people.

Amen.

Four

Mount Pisgah:
The Mountain of Hope

Then Moses climbed Mount Nebo from the plains of Moab to the top of Pisgah, across from Jericho. There the LORD showed him the whole land—from Gilead to Dan, all of Naphtali, the territory of Ephraim and Manasseh, all the land of Judah as far as the western sea, the Negev and the whole region from the Valley of Jericho, the City of Palms, as far as Zoar. Then the LORD said to him, "This is the land I promised on oath to Abraham, Isaac and Jacob when I said, 'I will give it to your descendants'"

(Deuteronomy 34:1–4)

A S A YOUNG BOY, IT WAS NOT AT ALL UNUSUAL FOR ME TO go to sleep at night with the full awareness that Jesus might well return for His Church during the night—especially on a Sunday night. You see, in the services on Sunday—both morning and evening— there was frequent mention of the "soon coming of Jesus." My dad would often preach about it. We, the congregation, would often sing, "He's coming soon, He's coming soon."[7] Each testimony service (when congregants told of their experience with the Lord) would be peppered with references to "the soon coming of Christ." At every turn there were forceful reminders that "this world is not my home." Such geopolitical events as the recent re-establishment of Israel as a nation and the alignment of Middle Eastern nations against Israel added great impetus to this "end times" preoccupation within my church tradition.

Jesus' promise to His disciples would certainly be fulfilled, and it would most likely happen before I got very far along in life! How often I would hear repeated in children's and youth services: "Go no place that you would not want to be found when Jesus comes. Do nothing you would not want to be caught doing when Jesus comes. Say nothing you would not want to be saying when Jesus comes."

There were some appropriate outcomes to the focus on the Second Coming of Christ in our theology. I will highlight those later. Such a preoccupation with the coming of Christ, however, tended to misdirect on two counts:

1) It fostered a negative motivation to the believer's walk—live righteously to avoid retribution.
2) It distracted us from a Biblical sense of responsibility to demonstrate the love of Christ in the midst of current culture.

I'm reminded of the startling scene as Jesus ascends from the earth, as recorded in Acts 1. The disciples were quite naturally taken aback by what they were observing and were straining their necks to view the event. The words of the angel provide an appropriate perspective. The question *"Why stand ye gazing?"* (Acts 1:11 KJV) may well be applied to much of twentieth century evangelicalism. Much time and effort have been devoted to teaching, preaching, and prodding on the subject of the Second Coming without a counterbalance of focus on the need to acknowledge the life and power of Christ being lived out in this present world.

But the same angel did declare, *"This same Jesus, who has been taken from you into heaven, will come back in the same way you have seen him go into heaven"* (Acts 1:11). So it would be also wrong to de-emphasize the fact of Christ's return. I find as I look around today that this too is a plank that has woefully weakened in today's Church. The pendulum has swung from overemphasis to virtual exclusion. An on-line sermon bank I sometimes visit boasts some 30,000 sermon titles, of which less than 0.02 percent deal with the Second Coming of Christ. How many churches might you visit this Sunday where you would have a good chance of hearing a sermon on the imminent return of Jesus? Our focus has almost exclusively come to be placed on this present world as opposed to the world to come.

Paul the apostle often found opportunity to draw a distinction between this present life and the life to come. Here is his comment to the troubled church at Corinth: *"If only for this life we have hope in Christ, we are to be pitied more than all men"* (1 Corinthians 15:19). Have we in the western church become contented with our affluent lifestyle to the point that heaven has lost its lustre?

As I compare my life today with that of my parents and their congregants, I can see why heaven would hold a greater attraction for them. Life was hard in the fifties and sixties in rural Newfoundland. The absence of plumbing, heating, and refrigeration—things we take for granted today—presented numerous challenges. Meat and fish had to be preserved by salting, clothes had to be hand washed and dried outdoors, and fuel had to be acquired from a woodlot. We tend to romanticize those times as "the good old days," but life was difficult and resources were limited. It is easy, therefore, to understand the desire to escape and go to a better place. But to emphasize the Second Coming as the hope of the Church is not an anti-biblical position. Paul gives a ringing endorsement of Christ's coming as the hope of the believer:

> It [the grace of God] teaches us to say "No" to ungodliness and worldly passions, and to live self-controlled, upright and godly lives in this present age, while we wait for the blessed hope—the glorious appearing of our great God and Savior, Jesus Christ (Titus 2:12,13).

The Promised Land In View

So the end of the journey for Moses is predictably eventful. His most remarkable life has been accented by mountaintop experiences of a supernatural kind. Now the Lord has come to him again to take him up another mountain—Mt. Pisgah, from which he will be able to view the Promised Land. For forty years he has led a stubborn and rebellious people through cycles of wilderness journeyings—a people who rightly deserve to remain trapped in that wilderness. From the complaints concerning the manna (Numbers 11:6) to the worshipping of the golden calf (Exodus 32:1–24), from the wails of dissatisfaction at Meribah (Exodus 17:1–7) to the negative report from ten of twelve spies (Numbers 13,14), there have been sufficient displays of unbelief for the Israelites to have been written off. Yes, from a human perspective the whole forty-year saga could be viewed as a failed experiment. But now God, in another overwhelming display of mercy, is repeating the promise to Moses:

> Then the LORD said to him, "This is the land I promised on oath to Abraham, Isaac and Jacob when I said, 'I will give it to your descendants.' I have let you see it with your eyes, but you will not cross over into it." And Moses the servant of the LORD died there in Moab, as the LORD had said. He buried him in Moab, in the valley opposite Beth Peor, but to this day no one knows where his grave is. Moses was a hundred and twenty years old when he died, yet his eyes were not weak nor his strength gone (Deuteronomy 34:4–7).

While Moses himself would not make it to Canaan, he would have the satisfaction of knowing that his faithful service during the past forty years was not in vain. God would fulfill His word and deliver His people to their promised destination. God's people are people on a journey, and it must never be forgotten that we are very much en route towards a certain destiny—a life whose promise far exceeds anything we could hope to experience in our current time-and-space existence.

But I've heard it said on more than one occasion, and by persons of varying ages, "Heaven doesn't hold much attraction for me, because there's so much about it that's unknown." Randy Alcorn, who has written an extensive volume on the positive features of heaven, addresses the affects of "unnatural" and unbiblical perspectives about how heaven may be perceived:

> When Heaven is portrayed as beyond the reach of our senses, it doesn't invite us; instead, it alienates us and even frightens us. Our misguided attempts to make Heaven "sound spiritual" (i.e., non-physical) merely succeed in making Heaven unappealing.[8]

It is true that the Bible only gives us glimpses of the reality of the life-after-life existence. While that is true, my faith in the Lord who has made us assures me that our joy, our discovery, and our creativity will know no limits. Alcorn believes that God has prepared a fascinating destination for His children.

> When I anticipate my first glimpse of Heaven, I remember the first time I went snorkelling. I saw countless fish of every shape, size and color. And just when I thought I'd seen the most beautiful fish, along came another even more striking. Etched in my memory is a certain sound—the sound of a gasp going through my rubber snorkel as my eyes were opened to that breathtaking underwater world. I imagine our first glimpse of Heaven will cause us to similarly gasp in amazement and delight.[9]

For Moses though, it was not so much the destination but the Presence that made the difference for him. Remember his prayer *If your Presence does not go with us, do not send us up from here* (Exodus 33:15). Moses, who had experienced the amazing impact of the Lord's presence, was more concerned about being with the

Lord than anything else. His moment of destiny was approaching in a different way. He would die, and the Lord would take care of his burial.

I have to say that this encounter with my Lord—the fact that I will experience His presence in a dimension I have not yet realized—is the single most important aspect of the Lord's coming for me. I will see Him! My mind goes back to many a Sunday morning service when as a boy I would enter into the spirit of the song chosen by my dad or my mom for that service.

> When all my labours and trials are o'er,
> And I am safe on that beautiful shore,
> Just to be near the dear Lord I adore,
> Will through the ages be glory for me.
>
> When by the gift of His infinite grace,
> I am accorded in heaven a place,
> Just to be there and to look on His face,
> Will through the ages be glory for me.
>
> Friends will be there I have loved long ago,
> Joy like a river around me will flow;
> Yet, just a smile from my Savior I know,
> Will through the ages be glory for me.[10]

Then the refrain, "When by His grace, I shall look on His face..." The song still evokes within me a passionate desire to experience that moment. Breathtaking, mind-boggling, self-effacing—it will be phenomenal. And to think that from that moment on I will be with Him! We sang the song at my dad's funeral. Thirteen years later, we sang a similar hymn at my mom's, reminiscent of those Sunday morning song services a generation ago.

> The song still evokes within me a passionate desire to experience that moment. Breathtaking, mind-boggling, self-effacing—it will be phenomenal. And to think that from that moment on I will be with Him!

When my life's work is ended
and I cross the swelling tide;
When the bright and glorious morning I shall see;
I shall know my Redeemer
When I reach the other side,
And His smile will be the first to welcome me.

Through the gates to the city
In a robe of spotless white,
He will lead me where no tears shall ever fall.
In the glad song of ages I will mingle with delight,
But I long to meet my Savior first of all.[11]

They were appropriate choices. It had been their lifelong pursuit. Their legacy to me and my family is this incomparable, incredible hope.

The wonder of this great hope which we embrace as believers is also captured in the more contemporary song by Mercy Me, "I Can Only Imagine." It addresses the wonder of the moment when we stand in His presence as it poses the question,

Surrounded by Your glory,
What will my heart feel?

Here, as in the traditional hymns, there is something that ought to be in the heart and mind of the Christian believer—a fascination, a positive and appropriate fascination, with the Person of Christ. Are you and I still struck by the wonder of Christ's love and affection for us? The apostle Paul's heartbeat was Christ alone. *"What is more, I consider everything a loss compared to the surpassing greatness of knowing Christ Jesus my Lord, for whose sake I have lost all things. I consider them rubbish, that I may gain Christ"* (Philippians 3:8). So it again comes down to a heart check, doesn't it? If I'm consumed with the wonder of Christ and His love for me, the greatest moment of my future will be to behold Him "face to face."

Yes, we experience His presence now and know His favour on a daily basis. But there ought to be a healthy anticipation and a balanced perception of the coming of the Lord. The early Church, focused on the reality of His return, would often use the greeting *Maranatha*, "the Lord is coming." Should not we, as we see the day approaching, give due attention to our "Promised Land" experience—the glorious return of Jesus Christ? I have to say that I really do wonder about a church culture that perpetually avoids any mention of Christ's return or our going to be with Him. Of course there are excesses when it comes to the prognostications of "Bible prophecy experts." The Church has been "burned" repeatedly by date setters and doomsayers. Maybe that's why we seem to see such intentional avoidance of a theology of heaven. Nonetheless, a Church that's in love with Jesus is a Church that will speak longingly and expectantly of our ultimate union with Him. The *"blessed hope—the glorious appearing"* (Titus 2:13) is as relevant to today's Church as it was to the Church of my youth. It is proper for us to cling to that hope in the same way that my father's generation did. The "plank" of hope, once restored, will ensure an appropriate focus on matters of destiny.

Let's pray the following prayer with full sincerity.

Dear Lord, as I look at my life and my preoccupation with things temporal, I become acutely aware of my need to dwell more intently on the hope that You have given Your Church—the promise that You will come again and that where You are, there we also shall be (John 14:3). I have esteemed too highly the things that shall pass away. The result is that my heart does not beat with joy and anticipation at the thought of Your coming.

Forgive me and draw near to me as I endeavour to draw near to You. Become once again the delight of my soul that You once were and restore to me again a healthy fascination for the moment when I shall see You face to face.

Let this awareness be rediscovered by the Church of Jesus in this land. Let the glory of Your presence fill Your house again so that nothing eclipses the beauty of Your face. And may we, Your Church, maintain a healthy desire to be in Your presence forever. May your servant David's cry genuinely become our cry. *"One thing have I desired of the LORD, that will I seek after; that I may dwell in the house of the LORD all the days of my life, to behold the beauty of the LORD, and to enquire in his temple"* (Psalm 27:4 KJV). Let this be the collective desire of Your Church, motivated not simply by a need to escape from this world but the desire to be in the purity, the holiness, the peace, and the security of Your presence forever.

Amen.

FIVE

Mount Carmel:
The Mountain of Faith

"Now summon the people from all over Israel to meet me on Mount Carmel. And bring the four hundred and fifty prophets of Baal and the four hundred prophets of Asherah, who eat at Jezebel's table"…"Answer me, O LORD, answer me, so these people will know that you, O LORD, are God, and that you are turning their hearts back again." Then the fire of the LORD fell and burned up the sacrifice

(1 Kings 18:19,37,38).

WHILE SOME OF MY FAVOURITE CHILDHOOD MEMO-ries involve outdoor adventure, there were also important and memorable family times—like when we would sit together prior to bed-time and listen to our parents tell stories of faith encounters in their earlier years of ministry. Mom would tell of the time shortly after they had arrived and set up home in a remote community, having no means of support and unable to rely on family or friends. One evening they had absolutely nothing for supper. So, together my mom and dad got down on their knees to pray that the Lord would provide food. While they were praying there was a knock at the door. A gentleman from the community had come with pro-visions—not just for the evening meal but sufficient for days to come! Dad would tell of how he was called on one dark night by a distressed father to come to his home where his young son had swallowed an opener key, having a sharp protruding tin edge, from a meat-loaf can. The normal thing to do in such a crisis was to call on the pastor to come and pray. There was no 911 to call—no emergency measures service and no readily available medical services. The prayer of faith was the first line of rescue. On this particular occasion the little boy vomited up the key as soon as my dad prayed. Such stories of faith were not uncommon and served to instill in me an understanding that *"The eyes of the LORD are upon the righteous, and his ears are open unto their cry"* (Psalm 34:15 KJV). The practice of coming to God in faith when there were needs in our own lives became the norm for us. We understood God to be ever-present—ever aware of our need for His touch and His provision.

Any such faith encounter is an opportunity to demonstrate Christ's power and love in the face of natural and, in some cases, demonic forces that war against the ways of God. The thing to remember is this: We don't try to create opportunities to grandstand the works of God's love and grace. The Word of God warns us not to put God to the test. David mentions this: *"They willfully put God to the test by demanding the food they craved"* (Psalm 78:18). Similarly, Jesus issues a warning from the Scriptures as He resists the temptations of the devil: *"Jesus answered him, 'It is also written: "Do not put the Lord your God to the test"'"* (Matthew 4:7). So let's be careful that we don't promote the kind of ill-advised showdowns wherein some have foolishly attempted to force the hand of God.

Nevertheless, over and over in the Scriptures we are reminded that God delights to have His children come to Him in faith. In fact the Bible tells us that without faith it is impossible to please Him (Hebrews 11:6). My concern, as we contemplate the need for a new level of qualitative faith in today's Church, is the number among us who might tend to be like the disciples who were amazed at Jesus' power and authority over the Galilean wind and waves, prompting His rebuke *"O you of little faith"* (Matthew 8:26 NKJV). The issue of faith comes down to your and my confidence in the living, ever-present Christ who is faithful to His Word—a God who does answer prayer.

> The issue of faith comes down to your and my confidence in the living, ever-present Christ who is faithful to His Word—a God who does answer prayer.

The Big Picture "Showdown"

As Elijah prepared for the dramatic showdown on Mt. Carmel, however, there was more at stake than simply the opportunity to witness an answer to the prayer of a man of God. At issue was the fact that the people of God had walked away from the path of obedience and faith in the God of their forefathers. They had adopted instead the practices of Baalism, resulting in the absence of any acquaintance with the true and living God. The burden of Elijah's heart was to convince his people that the God of Abraham, Isaac, and Jacob was the one true God. Elijah demonstrated zero tolerance for acceptance of the ways of Baal, and his objective was quite clearly to expose the fallacy of the religion that had infiltrated the minds and hearts of the Israelites.

> *When he saw Elijah, he said to him, "Is that you, you troubler of Israel?" "I have not made trouble for Israel," Elijah replied. "But you and your father's family have. You have abandoned the Lord's commands and have followed the Baals. Now summon the people from all over Israel to meet me on Mount Carmel. And bring the four hundred and fifty prophets of Baal and the four hundred prophets of Asherah, who eat at Jezebel's table"* (1 Kings 18:17–19).

It was a defining moment in which the people would be called to repent of deserting their God and to return with their whole hearts to the Lord.

It seems to us incredulous that the people of God so often turned from the Lord and adopted the religious viewpoints and practices of the surrounding peoples. How easily they allowed themselves to be assimilated into the dominant religions of neighbouring cultures! There must be a solid line of demarcation between the Church and the world. Baalism can never be tolerated in any form. As I reflect on the possible relevance of the Mt. Carmel episode to the Christian Church of today, I see an unfortunate parallel. In our democracy we place high value on the freedom of religion, and rightly so. Anyone, anywhere, in our Western democracies has the right to pursue his or her religion of choice without fear of interference or restriction. Christianity, in its various forms, enjoys this precious liberty. What then could be the negative comparison with the people of Elijah's day? The answer, as I see it, is pluralism and its powerful influence on the minds and hearts of the people of God.

What is pluralism and what is the challenge that it poses to members of the Church of Jesus Christ—those who desire to defend the exclusivity of the Christian message? Let's allow one of the foremost thinkers in the Church today to assist us in grasping the nature and enormity of the challenge. In 2003 Gary Barnes, associate director for the 2004 Lausanne Forum on World Evangelization, asked John Stott, former rector of All Souls, Langham Place, London, what he believed to be some of the most critical issues needing to be addressed by the working groups preparing for the 2004 forum. Here in part is Stott's answer:

> I focus on what to me is the most critical issue, and that is the challenge of pluralism. Pluralism is not just recognition that there is a plurality of faiths in the world today. That is an obvious fact. No, pluralism is itself an ideology. It affirms the independent validity of all faiths. It therefore rejects as arrogant and wholly unacceptable every attempt to convert anybody (let alone everybody) to our opinions.[13]

Those of us who have grown up with the idea that there are certain essentials that are uncompromisingly entrenched in our belief structure can hardly conceive that the message of the uniqueness of Christ would be called into question by Christians. We have serious difficulty accepting any suggestion that the exclusivity of salvation through Him would even be a point of discussion at all among evangelicals. We may therefore rightly be alarmed at the findings of George Barna as he has surveyed today's Church on this very question. As recently as 2005 Barna found that about one-third of "born agains" (33 percent) believe that if a person is "good enough" he or she can earn a place in heaven. He further found that only 32 percent of born agains said they believe in moral absolutes.[14] Barna also noted, from findings of another survey done in 2002, "Our continuing research among teenagers and adolescents shows that the trend away from adopting biblical theology in favor of syncretic, culture-based theology is advancing at full gallop."[15] These findings indicate to me that a significant segment of today's Church has absorbed the world view of the popular culture, and, correspondingly, we are guilty of abandoning our traditionally uncompromising adherence to Biblical dogma. John Stott elaborated on his professed concern about this troubling trend:

> The reason we must reject this increasingly popular position is that we are committed to the uniqueness of Jesus (he has no competitors) and his finality (he has no successors). It is not the uniqueness of "Christianity" as a system that we defend, but the uniqueness of Christ. He is unique in his incarnation (which is quite different from the ahistorical and plural "avatars" of Hinduism); in his atonement (dying once for all for our sins); in his resurrection (breaking the power of death); and in his gift of the Spirit (to indwell and transform us). So, because in no other person but Jesus of Nazareth did God first become human (in his birth), then bear our sins (in

his death), then conquer death (in his resurrection) and then enter his people (by his Spirit), he is uniquely able to save sinners. Nobody else has his qualifications.[16]

I find it interesting how Stott brings us back to the single defining reality of the Christian faith: the person of the Lord Jesus Christ. On each mountain—Moriah, Sinai, Pisgah, and now Carmel—as we juxtapose each scenario against the Church, we find that fundamentally it is all about Christ. Our greatest need is to make way for Christ in His fullness and essence to be reinstated in His Church.

So, on Mt. Carmel Elijah championed a showdown that was essentially a very public collision of faiths. At issue was the reliability and supremacy of the God of Israel versus the legitimacy of the worship of Baal.

So, on Mt. Carmel Elijah championed a showdown that was essentially a very public collision of faiths. At issue was the reliability and supremacy of the God of Israel versus the legitimacy of the worship of Baal. And so I say with all sincerity that we must see again a vigorous defence of the faith in the public domain. Church leaders must see their responsibility to align the voice of the Church with the essentials of God's Word and strengthen the faith of believing Christians by resisting the godless philosophy of pluralism. They must state and restate the exclusivity of Christ as the only Way to God!

This battle needs to be waged particularly where children and youth are concerned. The vast majority of "churched" kids live their lives in a predominantly anti-Christian environment—the world of public education, an environment that is totally sold out to the pluralistic world view. Josh McDowell is known for his observations and insights concerning the "churched" youth culture. He states:

> Today's youth seem to be just as interested in God and just as passionate about spiritual things as any generation. For more than a decade, young people have been the most spiritually interested individuals in America. Their interest is not in question at all. But the fundamental question is: "How are they forming their view of God? And what brand of religion are they adopting?"

- 63% don't believe Jesus is the Son of the one true God.
- 58% believe all faiths teach equally valid truths.
- 51% don't believe Jesus rose from the dead.
- 65% don't believe Satan is a real entity.
- 68% don't believe the Holy Spirit is a real entity.[17]

Reflecting again on my own childhood, I remember how my world view was forged by my parents and other adults who modelled and taught the ways of God. My concept of God, my commitment to Christ alone, and my understanding of the reliability of the changeless, objective truth of God's Word were engrained in my thinking through the example and the direct intentional teaching of the significant adults in my life. Our responsibility is to demonstrate before children the knowledge of Christ and His sacrifice for sin, to boldly declare that He alone is the way to God.

Let's not be afraid to put the truth concerning Christ, and the experience of knowing Him by grace through faith, up against the lame philosophies of our time. Let's not hesitate to build our altar by being explicit in our instruction concerning who Jesus is. Then, let us also be careful, applying the Word of God in every circumstance, to prevent the eruption of any fire that is not of God. Then let us ask Him to let the fire from Heaven fall again! The "God who answers by fire" will honour yet again to such a bold demonstration of faith. He will respond to the strong assertion of His singular right to be worshipped and glorified in our witness by demonstrating the fire of His presence in His Church.

How strong, how securely positioned is the plank of faith in the Church today? How firmly positioned is faith in your life and experience? Elijah is the key player on Mt. Carmel, a giant of faith and power...

Wait!—The apostle James seems to indicate that he was an ordinary man: *"Elijah was a man just like us"* (James 5:17). His distinguishing characteristic was his willingness to be vulnerable and to put his whole life on the line so that the power and greatness of God might be displayed. Do you—or the members of your family or the members of your church—need to have your faith restored in the God of Abraham, Isaac, and Jacob? Let's go to the mountain of faith and allow Him to demonstrate His power once again. Would you join me in asking the Lord to show His power in our time?

Dear Lord, for too long we've observed the gradual but definite incursion of error and deceit into the thinking of Your people, the Church. We have watched as the enemy of our souls has sought to erode the essentials of Bible truth from the minds and hearts of those who are called by Your Name. We have allowed the universalistic world view of our popular culture to become acceptable and have failed to acknowledge the effect such godless views have had on our children and youth.

Embolden the pastors and teachers in Your Church, Your servants, to take seriously their responsibility to preach the whole gospel without compromise. Raise up new champions of the Christian faith. Empower them by Your Spirit to speak in plain, understandable terms concerning the exclusivity of Christ as the Way to God and the necessity for all people to be born again by the Spirit of God.

Forgive us and plant within us a renewed resolve to proclaim the exclusive message of salvation through Christ. Let the fire of Heaven fall upon us in such a way that we, our children, and our grandchildren will turn our hearts completely to Christ and His gospel so that our unwavering faith in His name will bear witness of His power and His grace.

I offer myself to You as a vessel through which You may demonstrate Your power. I build an altar of faith in my own life. Even amidst a society that scorns the notion of an exclusive view of salvation, I will stand for Your truth and will encourage the succeeding generation to repel pluralism and promote an uncompromising acceptance of the declared truths of Your Word.

May Your power within us enable us to have the resolve to stand true. I pray with faith in Jesus' strong name.

Amen.

Six

The Mount of the Transfiguration: The Mountain of Revelation

After six days Jesus took with him Peter, James and John the brother of James, and led them up a high mountain by themselves. There he was transfigured before them

(Matthew 17:2).

GROWING UP, AND EVEN TO THIS DAY, I HAVE HELD A love–hate regard for high mountains. There is a certain grandeur, a certain other-worldliness about high mountains—spectacular to view on the one hand but intimidating and dangerous on the other. While the mountains of Newfoundland fail to rival the towering Rockies of the west coast, the northern version of the great Appalachian chain are nonetheless rugged and overwhelming in their beauty. It was likely during my attempts to keep up with my bigger brother and his pals as they scaled the crags and minor hills of the island's rough terrain that I developed my acrophobia. I remember one day distinctly feeling tense—more accurately, frozen—while clinging to the edge of a precipice, afraid to go up or down. I was stuck there for some time but eventually mustered the courage to complete the climb. Such childhood experiences made me acquire a great respect for mountains. I love to view mountains, I love the view from mountains, but whenever I reach the top I have a gripping fear of the view straight down! Why do mountains hold my respect and interest in such a way? It might have something to do with the fact that they afford opportunity to rise above the normal rush of life, away from the limited vision of the lower levels.

High mountains are not readily accessed by the mainstream. They take you above the plane where the majority live, and they afford a perspective that can never be gained from the lower levels. My boyhood exploits often took me to vantage points from which I could spot small boats or, at times, ocean-going ships dwarfed by the vast expanse of blue ocean below. At other times I remember seeing houses, animals, and people like miniature pieces on a tabletop landscape, again rendered diminutive and sometimes imperceptible by the height. Mountains have a way of drastically influencing perspective.

The scriptural record states that Jesus took Peter, James, and John to a high mountain (Matthew 17:1). It's interesting to speculate why this particular detail is given. The place, chosen by God long before the event took place, would have to be well separated from the crowds, even from the majority of the disciples. The perspective of the three disciples on the plan and purpose of God was not to be affected by the view of what was below but by what took place right before their eyes on the mountain itself. It would nevertheless profoundly impact their perception of the world from that day on. The demonstration of God's glory that would occur on the mountain was certainly reserved for the exclusive experience of the three. Perhaps the long walk back down the mountain provided the opportunity needed to debrief and the time for Jesus to respond to the many questions that must have filled the minds of the disciples, especially Peter. One thing is certain—what took place on that mountain was of inestimable importance, for the disciples and for the Church they would help establish. They were taken far above the plane of normal living and were given a perspective that would alter their thinking for the rest of their days.

> One thing is certain—what took place on that mountain was of inestimable importance, for the disciples and for the Church they would help establish.

It is clear that Jesus was employing an important leadership dynamic of instructing a small, select group in an intimate setting so that they might later convey its significance to others. Each of the three would subsequently have notable impact in the launch of the Church. Each would be involved in bringing valued instruction to the Church. Peter was a chief instrument in the founding of the Church, preaching the first gospel sermon on the Day of Pentecost. James was a respected leader in the early Church. We see him taking a strong stand as he communicates the decision of the Jerusalem Council in Acts 15. John, "the beloved disciple," became the most prolific writer of New Testament truth. The lasting impact the experience had on Peter is evident in his own writings.

We did not follow cleverly invented stories when we told you about the power and coming of our Lord Jesus Christ, but we were eyewitnesses of his majesty. For he received honor and glory from God the Father when the voice came to him from the Majestic Glory, saying, "This is my Son, whom I love; with him I am well pleased." We ourselves heard this voice that came from heaven when we were with him on the sacred mountain (2 Peter 1:16–18).

Who Is Jesus to You?

In this survey of key mountains of the Bible we have named the Mount of Transfiguration *the mountain of revelation.* As we walk with Peter, James, and John through their experience on the mountain, we witness a sharp and intentional focus on Jesus. Jesus had assumed before their eyes a state of radiance—a brilliance that dramatically exhibited the glory of God (Matthew 17:2). Moses and Elijah appeared and spoke with Him (Matthew 17:3). Imagine the startled reaction of the disciples! Who would believe such a fantastic story? What could it all mean? Peter, for one, at the moment certainly didn't get it. The Matthew account indicates that he was totally overwhelmed by what he saw but missed the significance.

The religious tradition of those three had placed high value on the teachings of the Torah and the message of the prophets. Moses had been the recipient of the law on Mount Sinai and had been the one to proclaim the law to the people of God. Elijah had championed the cause of the God of Israel on Mount Carmel and was recognized as the first and greatest of the Old

Testament prophets. So we have for these Jewish men a fantastic occurrence, two icons representing the law and the prophets converging at one location. Moses, the author of the law; Elijah, representing the prophets; and Jesus, the great rabbi who had so expertly clarified many of the Scriptures to them—all together in one place! Who could ask for a more august gathering? With this in mind, we may be more apt to be forgiving of Peter for blurting out the thought of building three tabernacles—one for Jesus, one for Moses, and one for Elijah (Matthew 17:4). He knew

> We are prone to sanctify tradition and fail to observe the central, most important element, indeed the very essence of our faith—the Person of Christ.

enough to know that something of spiritual significance was taking place. "This has to be good! Let's savour the moment! Let's maximize the experience!"

What happens next blows Peter's suggestion out of the water. What Peter had uttered was representative of human tendency. We are prone to sanctify tradition and fail to observe the central, most important element, indeed the very essence of our faith—the Person of Christ. Here's Matthew's account of the moment:

> *While he was still speaking, a bright cloud enveloped them, and a voice from the cloud said, "This is my Son, whom I love; with him I am well pleased. Listen to him!" When the disciples heard this, they fell facedown to the ground, terrified. But Jesus came and touched them. "Get up," he said. "Don't be afraid." When they looked up, they saw no one except Jesus* (Matthew 17:5–8).

Judson Cornwall captures the truth concerning our natural inclination and says that amazingly the human heart quickly contents itself with something short of God and devises elaborate substitutes for Him.

> If we will accept the dictionary's definition of worship as, "to adore, to exalt, to magnify, to dote, to admire, to esteem," then it becomes quite obvious that many Christians worship, to a lesser extent perhaps, many things that are beneath the image of God. Some exalt their denomination in a manner that at least borders worship. Others dote dangerously on their pastor, while others magnify a doctrinal truth almost to the place of God Himself.[18]

The voice from the cloud thunders, "This is my one and only Son; listen to Him." So overwhelming was the experience it left all three recoiling on the ground in fear. How often we have seen such things as form and tradition replace our love and worship of Jesus Christ! For Peter, the tradition of the law and the prophets, personified at that moment in Moses and Elijah, came to the fore of his thinking, and he was ready to equate their presence with the Person of Christ. He was ready to ascribe a similar value and place to Moses and Elijah as to Jesus. The response from the Father was so direct and dramatic that it ought to give us pause. But you may well argue that we now are more enlightened than Peter was at the time. We understand that the essence of the message presented by the law and the prophets was a foreshadowing of the coming Christ. Peter lets us know that he gets it as he later writes:

> *Concerning this salvation, the prophets, who spoke*
> *of the grace that was to come to you, searched*
> *intently and with the greatest care, trying to find out*
> *the time and circumstances to which the Spirit of*
> *Christ in them was pointing when he predicted the*
> *sufferings of Christ and the glories that would*
> *follow. It was revealed to them that they were not*
> *serving themselves but you, when they spoke of the*
> *things that have now been told you by those who*
> *have preached the gospel to you by the Holy Spirit*
> *sent from heaven. Even angels long to look into these*
> *things* (1 Peter 1:10–12).

The fact is that the average evangelical believer understands this. No argument! What we fail to grasp though is that we, as Judson Cornwall attests, are apt to "devise elaborate substitutes." Is it possible that we are often more concerned about preserving our traditions than about honouring Christ? This question is particularly relevant to those of us who belong to the "boomer" generation. Our worship styles, our Sunday habits, our blind denominational loyalties, yes, and even such lofty ideals as our commitment to world missions can often elicit stronger emotions, more consistent dedication, than our devotion to the Lord Jesus Christ.

I have been in the presence of many who have displayed uncommon dedication to the idea of evangelizing the world. I have also often wondered to myself if the same individuals have a vital, living love for Jesus. The Christian gospel offers hope for the world. It offers a superior quality of living. It's easy to be enthusiastic about the pronouncement of its merits. But the penetrating question that comes to me and to you is this: *Do our lives display a depth of worship and an undying love for Christ?* The Holy Spirit's purpose is to bring Christ—His work and His Person—to the front and centre of our hearts. This is the message from the Mount of Transfiguration. This, I fear, represents a key missing plank from "the temple" of today. As a pastor in a large, busy church, I must ask myself the critical questions. Am I allowing my works of service—busyness in the Lord's work—to replace the cultivation of a vibrant relationship with Christ? Am I substituting the "practice" for the "presence"? The Mount of Transfiguration, the mountain of revelation, opens our eyes to a proper perspective regarding our centre of life and truth.

> Am I substituting the "practice" for the "presence"? The Mount of Transfiguration, the mountain of revelation, opens our eyes to a proper perspective regarding our centre of life and truth.

Of interest to me also, in keeping with the theme of this book, is what happens in the scene where the voice of God is heard. The cloud, a Biblical symbol of the presence of God, envelops all of them (Matthew 17:5). You see, when it comes to the great task of the ages—the evangelization of the world—Christ and His Church are inseparable. Instead of in the structure of the past, the physical tent, representing the dwelling place of God, He would from now on dwell within His people. His glory would be manifested in them!

Yes, this idea too was engrained in my thinking as I grew in my understanding of the Christian walk. Christ was to be *"all, and...in all"* (Colossians 3:11). The songs and testimonies in my parents' little church constantly reminded me of the all-sufficiency of Christ. The knowledge that "without Him I can do nothing" (see John 15:5) was purposefully driven home to my mind time and time again. Yet head knowledge of this wonderful truth is not enough. There must be a heart connect with the glorified Christ. Oswald J. Smith, founder of The Peoples Church in Toronto, gave powerful expression to this as he wrote from his own experience.

I have walked alone with Jesus
In a fellowship divine,
Never more can earth allure me,
I am His and He is mine.

On the mountain I have seen Him,
Christ my Comforter and Friend,
And the glory of that vision
Will be with me to the end.

I have seen Him; I have known Him,
For He deigns to walk with me,
And the glory of His presence
Will be mine eternally.

O the glory of His presence,
O the beauty of His face.
I am His and His forever.
He has won me by His grace.[19]

Oswald's daughter, Hope Evangeline, exhibiting something of that same passion, gives poetic expression to the words of the apostle Paul.

> For me to live is Christ,
> All else must pass away;
> The things for which I've striven
> Must vanish and decay.
> But He will never leave me.
> He changeless will remain.
> To live in Christ is glory;
> To die in Him is gain.

> For me to live is Christ,
> With Him I'm crucified;
> I live and yet not I
> In me He doth abide.
> For me to live is Christ,
> He's everything to me;
> For me to live is Christ
> For all eternity.[20]

So, let me repeat the question posed at the head of this section. Who is Jesus to you? Do you have that vital heart-to-heart connection with Him? At the same time, do you worship Him as the awesome God He is, distinct from any structures of the past and your cherished traditions? Ravi Zacharias, a giant among Christian apologists, has written a book he titles *Walking from East to West*. The book is an autobiography, and, in addition to stimulating the mind (as Ravi's writings always do), it achieves deep impact on the soul of the reader. In it Ravi makes a summative statement relating to the believer's walk with Christ.

> Through all the visitations of life—successes or failures—it is not how well you are known or not known. It is not how big your organization is or isn't. It is not even how many sermons one has preached or books one has written or millions of dollars one has accumulated. It is *how well do you know Jesus?* That's it. That is what shapes how you view everything else. Successes are hollow if you do not know the author of life and His purpose. To me, with each passing year, Jesus has only become more beautiful.[21]

On the mountain He quieted and reassured the disciples with His gentle voice and sensitive manner. Ever the meek and patient Saviour, He knocks at your heart's door and mine and seeks admission and communion (Revelation 3:20). How can I be so ungracious as to ignore His knocking, to turn aside from His call for fellowship with me? This is not a small thing! We must, in honest reflection, allow Ravi's question to be asked: "How well do you know Jesus?"

From Mountain to Mission

The walk down the mountain would likely have been interesting. Remember, it would have been a long walk, since it was a high mountain. Peter for sure would have been full of questions. All three most likely would have preferred to stay and prolong this fascinating episode in their walk with Christ. But descend the mountain they must. They must proceed from their *otherworld* experience to the *needy world awaiting them below*. You see, while there's work to be done we cannot stay on the mountain. It's worth noting that, once they descended into the realities of life at the base of the mountain, they were confronted with a desperate human situation—a helpless father trying to find

> He truly is Lord of all and can deliver the bound and the fearful from the tyranny of the enemy who dominates this world and holds people in despair.

healing for his demon-possessed son (Matthew 17:14–18). Jesus demonstrated in action what had been manifested in glorious splendour on the mountain. He truly is Lord of all and can deliver the bound and the fearful from the tyranny of the enemy who dominates this world and holds people in despair. The Church that knows Christ, that sees Him as the One who has all power over the enemy, is the Church that must confront the ills of our society with Christ's message of power and love.

The Church has no option but to confront human need on all fronts and, by God's grace, to proclaim a message of hope to those who are in distress. The first qualifying fact that Jesus gave to the disciples of John the Baptist when they were sent to inquire whether or not Jesus was the Christ was that the poor had the gospel preached to them (Luke 7:18–22). I recently spoke with a leader of a successful inner-city mission. He stated that the Church of the future will be defined by how it ministers to the poor. The Church, renewed by His presence, will have more than a passing concern for the plight of the poor.

Isn't it fair to say that the Church of today in many ways tends to make the same mistake as Peter did when he witnessed the glory of Christ? Do we not prefer to "build our tabernacles" and fail to undertake our duty to manifest the redeeming power of Christ to a world that's desperately lost? The poor—refugees, new immigrants, single mothers, the chronically unemployed— must see the compassion of Christ reflected in His Church. The Lord's glory will best be seen in me as I go from the mountain of His revealed majesty to the world for which He died. This means being willing to share life, the life that is Christ, with others. But how does this look in reality? I'm afraid it requires that we become incarnational in the truest sense.

When I was growing up in "outport" Newfoundland, the poor were not always easily identified. I guess in a way everyone could be classified as poor. Then too, there existed a fierce pride among the people so that others would never have been allowed to know just how needy a particular family might be. But there were times when families suffered lack for reasons of long periods of unemployment, low fish harvest, or simply, in the case of larger families, too many mouths to feed. One thing was very clear, however, when anyone was known to be in need, the community of believers took ownership of that need and provided sustenance and care to help alleviate the pain. As far as I know, no one went hungry and no one went cold. Widows, orphans, the infirm, and the less fortunate would have wood supplied for their wood-burning furnaces and stoves, meat donated from a recently slaughtered cow, moose, seal, or caribou, or groceries dropped off at the door without any expectation of repayment. Those in need became recipients of gifts of life from a caring community.

We can draw a marked contrast between this rural setting of yesteryear and the urban context of today. The Church has virtually abandoned the inner city, where there remains a concentration of deep human need. How can we share life with those from whom we've extricated our presence? The lesson we must take from the mountain of revelation is that to declare the Lord's glory—to manifest His character of kindness and grace—we cannot stay in isolation in our "tents of worship." We must be the extension of the hands of Christ, championing His cause by addressing the needs of the desolate. As modeled by Christ, the compassionate nature of the gospel must translate into a willingness to share our lives with the broken and hurting in our cities.

I must confess that I'm not exactly sure just what such "sharing of life" looks like. Perhaps the approach that Greg Paul has modeled for a number of years comes close to what Jesus expects of all of us. Greg is the director of Sanctuary, an inner-city ministry in the heart of Toronto. Greg and his family, along with a number of dedicated believers, don't commute in and out of the city like many who minister to the inner-city poor, but they develop community and live their lives within the inner-city culture. They live and work among those classified as society's rejects. Greg has written a book he titled *God in the Alley,* in which he aptly summarizes his approach to compassionate ministry.

> Being among people means being in their midst, not outside. It means being with them, not being over them. It means not looking away from their agony or humiliation, but beholding it, and having the courage to be wounded by their pain.[22]

Perhaps for you and me it is a simple matter of allowing the compassionate heart of Christ to be expressed right where we are—in our immediate neighbourhood or place of work. Kindness, concern, and caring are not complicated concepts. As we manifest Christ's love through caring for those nearby, who knows where He might lead us?

On the mountain the three disciples observed in Christ the transcendent nature of the glory of God. At the foot of the mountain the heart of God was manifested as Jesus reached out and ministered life and healing to a hurting people. The revelation of who Jesus is must be applied to the outworking of His love as we live our lives in His world. New Testament scholar N. T. Wright was interviewed by journalist Tim Stafford on the subject of how to present the gospel in a post-modern world. The following statement by Wright hits at the core of the issue:

> The key to mission is always worship. You can only be reflecting the love of God into the world if you are worshiping the God who creates the world out of self-giving love. The more you look at that God and celebrate that love, the more you have to be reflecting that overflowing love into the world.[23]

Let's ascend once again the mountain of revelation and see that the house of the Lord is reinforced with the timber that assures a renewed sense of reverence for who Jesus is. Let's demonstrate our worship by showing His compassion to the needy around us. If you're like me, you long to experience a fresh glimpse of the majesty of Christ and a fresh realization of His power within. I dare you to pray this prayer with me!

Dear Lord Jesus, I bow before You in worship and declare You to be the one and only Lord of my life. You transcend the attractions of this temporal life and the appeal of all this world offers me.

The account of the mountaintop experience of Peter, James, and John stirs within me a yearning for Your presence. I know the way of salvation, and I am committed to making it known. I know the importance of living according to Your precepts. I have been the benefactor as I have applied to my own life the principles of righteous living. I have been amazed at what You do as You live in me and work through me. I will continue to proclaim that You are the new and living way, the only name by which one may be saved. I am dedicated to upholding Your truth as I live and interact within Your Body, the Church.

But I long for a fresh glimpse of Your majesty. I yearn for a renewed vision of the exalted and glorified Christ. Come, Lord Jesus, and display Your glory in and through my life. Take away my affection for dead tradition and form. Do away with low expectations and limited perspective. Come, fill me to overflowing with Your holy presence so that I am compelled to go into Your world with eyes full of mercy and a heart that feels the pain and senses the lostness of others.

Amen.

SEVEN

Mount Calvary:
The Mountain of Sacrifice

And when they had come to the place called Calvary, there they crucified Him, and the criminals, one on the right hand and the other on the left

(Luke 23:33 NKJV).

I HAVE EARLIER MADE MENTION OF THE ADVANTAGES THAT came my way by virtue of being born into a pastor's home. There was a certain recognition that potentially translated into particular benefit depending on the circumstances. I recall Christmas gifts, favours at school (both in and out of the classroom), and other situations of advantage that, in retrospect, may have been directly related to my belonging to a pastor's family. But there also were some disadvantages—not many, but some. For one, it was never easy for my brothers or me to live in a fishbowl—especially when there was often a typical boyish tendency towards mischief. When the preacher's boys did something they shouldn't do, it became quickly known throughout the community. Sad to say, any semblance of righteous living on my part was more often imposed by this community dynamic than by the reality of a close walk with the Lord!

101

Another disadvantage was not readily seen but nonetheless real. From my earliest memories I was part of a family environment in which it seemed that my serving the Lord for life was a presupposition. The church services, the singing around the piano as my mother played, the nightly family prayers, the practice of faith in my home—all led me to believe that there was no other option for me in life but to be a follower of Jesus. Even as I started school, the publicly funded Christian school system meant that I was further indoctrinated (in a good way) at school to put Christ first in my life. The danger of course was the possibility of assuming that I was already forgiven and, hence, failing to come to grips with my personal responsibility to ask Christ to forgive my sins and be Lord of my life. I guess you could call it "salvation by osmosis." Thank the Lord He made it very clear to me in my early years that there can be no such thing.

A few short years ago Brenda and I made a trip back to the little town where I spent most of my growing-up years. We drove along what seemed now to be a very short road (it had seemed quite a long road when I was a boy) leading to the old school-house where I began my educational career. While the distances seemed much shorter and the hills much smaller, I was amazed, not only that the schoolhouse was still there, but at how little had changed. As I viewed the old building and its sur-roundings, many memories came alive. I noted the high rocky crag that we would jump from in winter into the deep snowdrifts below. I observed the steep hill adjacent to the school property that we would sled down at breakneck speed on those cold, sunny January days. The woodlot where we would invent all manner of imaginary schemes and pursuits was still there! So much seemed to be as it used to be that names and faces of some decades past were momentarily reborn in my mind.

After some time of my private reminiscing we got back into the car and began to head back to the main road. I paused to look closely as we passed a spot that holds enormous significance in my life to this day. The little church building was no longer there, but the location was unmistakable to me. After all, it was the place where the single most important decision of my life was made. In my early childhood years much of my life was centred on what took place in that little white church building. It was the place where the people of the community gathered faithfully three times every Sunday—for the morning worship service, the afternoon Sunday school, and the evening service. It was the place where my dad preached and where my mom played the piano and, from time to time, gave her life story of how God had led her from her youth. It was the place where I would hear of the Lord's dealings in the lives of the people as they gave their testimonies—testimonies generally riddled with clichés and repetition. Nevertheless, the whole experience—the atmosphere, the culture—served to impress upon me the notion that the walk of faith was the only way to journey through this life. Since I was immersed in such a culture of faith from my earliest memories, it would take a work of God's Spirit to bring me to an understanding that I was a sinner in need of the cleansing power of the blood of Christ to wash away my sin.

"The Open Session"

Sunday afternoon at three o'clock the desk bell would ring on the pulpit at the front of the little church auditorium, marking the beginning of the day's Sunday school session. The children, and the few adults attending, would belt out all four verses of "Bringing in the Sheaves," or some other similar song, and then classes would begin. The classes consisted of rearranged pews, creating circles for the various age groups. Sound barriers of any kind between the groups were non-existent, so, five minutes in, we had a situation of organized confusion as each group leader competed against the noise coming from the rest of the room. It's a wonder any learning took place, but it did! The flannel-graph-supported lessons were effective in conveying Bible stories and Bible truths in spite of the noise factor.

> My love for Christ then, and my growing love for Him today, is a response to His incredible act of love for me.

My favourite Sunday school session was called the "open session." It was a time once a month when all the classes would merge to hear a story or watch a special program at the front of the auditorium. One January Sunday my mom was leading the open session and gave an explanation of the cross of Jesus. She explained, in words I had heard before, how we each must make a personal response to what Christ has done for us and individually receive Him into our hearts as Saviour and

Lord. On finishing the lesson she gave an invitation for any boys or girls who had never given their lives to Jesus to come forward and kneel. That afternoon, with an impact that was compelling and memorable, the Holy Spirit made me acutely aware that Jesus had died for me and that I need to personally give my life to Him. I, without any prompting from my siblings or friends, went forward, knelt, and confessed my sins to God. I was six years old, and the significance of what took place at that moment of my life has never left me. My love for Christ then, and my growing love for Him today, is a response to His incredible act of love for me.

The Sacrifice Foretold

A bird's-eye view of Mt. Moriah (our "mountain of obedience") where Abraham had taken Isaac to build an altar and sacrifice him to God shows that the hill of Calvary where Jesus was crucified is located just a little to the northwest. Just as we may look and see the geographical proximity of the two elevations, we may also look back historically and see how the two events connect. Remember Isaac's heart-wrenching question, *"Father...where is the lamb for the burnt offering?"* Abraham's response, *"God himself will provide the lamb,"* was powerfully prophetic. It came to partial fulfillment when the voice of God intercepted Abraham's agonizing act (Genesis 22:6–12). It was as if God were saying, "No, Abraham, you don't have to give your son as a sacrifice to Me; I'll give My Son as a sacrifice for you."

As mentioned already, *Moriah* means "forseen of God" meaning that God had deliberately chosen this place. Long before Abraham—long before Adam—God

105

in His amazing love and mercy had determined that His Son, Jesus Christ, would die for my sins and the sins of the world. In Revelation 13:8 Jesus is called *"the Lamb slain from the foundation of the world"* (NKJV). This determinant will and counsel of God, sending His Son to be the required sacrifice for sin, is etched in His plan as revealed throughout the pages of the Old Testament. His incomparable plan of substitution is woven throughout the tapestry of Old Testament law and ritual. We see it in the slaying of an unblemished lamb at the time of the Passover. We see it in the spotless lambs, bulls, and goats of the temple offerings. We see it in the outlay of the temple. We hear it consistently proclaimed through the words of the psalms and the prophets. We also read it, poignantly described, in the message of Isaiah: *"He was wounded for our transgressions, He was bruised for our iniquities; The chastisement for our peace was upon Him, And by His stripes we are healed"* (Isaiah 53:5 NKJV). Substitution, what an incredible truth—so wonderful that many fail to receive it—that God Himself would offer His Son to take upon Himself the horror and the penalty of my sin! This remarkable truth brings to mind another song from my childhood—still sung (by some) today.

> And can it be that I should gain
> An interest in the Savior's blood?
> Died He for me, who caused His pain—
> For me, who Him to death pursued?
> Amazing love! How can it be
> That Thou, my God, shouldst die for me?[24]

Yes, I have learned to look upon the crucifixion of Christ as the single most cherished and important event of history. It is the one event that impacts my life today far more profoundly than anything else does. Paul the apostle grasped the extraordinary weight of it in his writings. Paul was an educated, sophisticated former Jewish rabbi and Sanhedrin ruler. He was a man who was blessed with superior intelligence and a strong motivation to excel. Without a doubt Paul was one of the most dominant personalities of the New Testament era and had become one of the most renowned leaders in the Church. Paul had written the majority of the epistles. He was a church planter extraordinaire, founding more churches than any other apostle did. He had travelled countless miles in missionary journeys into uncharted territory. He overcame more setbacks and hardship than any other apostle and had phenomenal spiritual experiences and spiritual power in his life. Today's Church would laud Paul as the great superstar of the Christian faith. Yet Paul's attitude would be "No red carpet for me!" Instead, he emphatically stated that the only thing he found worth bragging about was *the cross of our Lord Jesus Christ* (Galatians 6:14). Paul said, "If I will do any bragging at all, it will be in the cross of Jesus Christ!" Paul got it. He understood the enormity of it.

Yes, I have learned to look upon the crucifixion of Christ as the single most cherished and important event of history. It is the one event that impacts my life today far more profoundly than anything else does.

The Cross in Today's Church

In my growing-up years, if ever there was a saturation of a point of doctrine, it would have to be the message of the cross. The redeeming work of Christ was the theological centre of everything. It was sung, preached, and taught—taught, preached, and sung—over and over and over. Here are some of the song titles that I grew up knowing well and that rush readily to my mind when I think of the subject of the cross: "The Old Rugged Cross," "At Calvary," "Burdens Are Lifted at Calvary," "Calvary Covers It All," "In the Cross of Christ I Glory," "Wounded for Me," "Were You There When They Crucified My Lord?"—the list is endless. It was impossible to grow up in the atmosphere I did and miss the significance of the message of Christ's sacrifice. It was my mom's message on that historic afternoon when I walked to the front and knelt to receive Him as my Saviour. It was that same message that impacted the lives of many other children in my mom's ministry. To reject Christ was to knowingly turn your back on unparalleled love, displayed so convincingly through the sacrifice He made at Calvary.

It could be argued that my experience represented an overemphasis on the message of the cross to the exclusion of more practical teaching of life lessons. Be that as it may, it begs the question "What is the experience of children who are growing up in today's Church?" It seems that "being relevant" is a primary value in the Church of today. Unfortunately, the message of the cross is perceived as being hardly relevant to a society that places such a high premium on maintaining the optics of a "together" life. The facade we all like to wear is that we are in control. We maintain that facade through such disciplines as employing business smarts, staying informed, maintaining a positive work ethic, and focusing all our energies and technical skills on our chosen career paths. Brokenness and deep need don't mesh well with what our society values. We prefer to sanitize the reality of the fact that we are

> Today's preaching weighs heavily on the side of what we can do to make life better instead of *what Christ has done to give us real life.*

"undone" (Isaiah 6:5 NKJV). Yet, we are indeed broken and sinful people and we are in deep need, and that's where the message of the cross brings hope and liberty!

Today's culture needs to hear the message of forgiveness and cleansing. Yet the most popular Sunday morning sermon is the one that encourages the hearers to apply certain work or friendship dynamics to get the most meaning out of life. Today's preaching weighs heavily on the side of what we can do to make life better instead of *what Christ has done to give us real life.* And what a lopsided exchange it is! He was condemned that I might be forgiven. He was rejected that I might be accepted. He was crucified that I might be justified! He was bound that I might be free. He was Jesus, so prone to retreat into the shadows, so loathe to see Himself acclaimed as the peoples' champion—now lifted up for all to see—marred and bleeding so that I might know forgiveness, dignity, and purpose. This, the theme of some of the giants of revival movements in relatively recent Church history—the Wesleys, Charles Finney, William Booth, D. L.

Moody, R. A. Torrey—ought to be the primary theme of today's pulpit.

Perhaps today's pastors and teachers ought to spend a little more time climbing Mount Calvary to re-examine the work of the cross than visiting yet another seminar on leadership. Some time ago I wrote a short article on the subject of leadership, and I recently reviewed the words that I wrote:

> The writer to the Hebrews invites us to consider Him *"who for the joy that was set before Him..."* (Hebrews 12:1,2 NKJV). When He laid down His life, He saw well into the future. The joy set before Him included your salvation and mine. And so I see other marks of leadership—true marks of leadership—as I gaze upon Him. I see the scars in His brow representing the thorns that pierced it and drew blood—His pure, cleansing blood that purchased my redemption. I see the lacerations on His back representing the scourging that He so willing endured. I see the nail prints in His hands that represent the nails that pinned Him to the cross on which He died for you and me.
>
> I hear Him say *"Father, forgive them, for they know not what they do"* (Luke 23:34 KJV).
>
> And I respond, with the words of Thomas as he touched the Saviour's wounds, *"My Lord and my God!"* (John 20:28).

What an unequalled example Jesus provides us of strength and of devotion to a calling. I fully understand that Jesus' purpose in dying was not primarily to be an example but to pay the penalty for sin. His sacrifice for me means that no other sacrifice is required. *"But when the kindness and love of God our Savior appeared, he saved us, not because of righteous things we had done, but because of his mercy"* (Titus 3:4,5). I also realize that He said, *"If anyone would come after me, he must deny himself and take up his cross daily and follow me"* (Luke 9:23). So there is an expectation that I, knowing the total abandon Christ exhibited on my behalf, will respond in kind.

Again, as I reflect upon the distant past, another oft-repeated song springs to my mind:

> Must Jesus bear the cross alone,
> And all the world go free?
> No, there's a cross for everyone,
> And there's a cross for me.[25]

But how does this "cross bearing" translate into my day-to-day living? Perhaps Paul's statement assists us in understanding what it's about. *"May I never boast except in the cross of our Lord Jesus Christ, through which the world has been crucified to me, and I to the world"* (Galatians 6:14). If Christ's cross has meant that the world has been *"crucified to me, and I to the world,"* the way in which I regard the things of the world will be dramatically altered. I believe it's fair to say that, in light of Calvary, the majority of North American believers fail to place the world in its right perspective. We are allured and driven by this world's values. We don't like to admit it, but many of us are more tuned into the stock market than we are to the suffering and lost humanity for whom Christ died. Yes, without too much argument, I think we would all readily admit that the plank of sacrifice for the sake of the Kingdom of God has significantly weakened in our time.

The Cross and Mission

A song (I can hear it now) often sung at the end of the Sunday evening service when I was a boy contained the following words: "How can I make a lesser sacrifice, when Jesus gave His all?"[26] Such sacrificial love requires a like response from my heart and life. It is the compelling message of extreme love that motivated missionaries of past years to go to remote destinations without any expectation of returning home. Moravian missionaries for centuries provide an example of that kind of high-risk (from a purely natural perspective) dedication to Christ.

I was born close to a part of the world where such surrender was played out with considerable daring and cost. You would be hard pressed to find a more harsh winter climate than that of Labrador, the "mainland" section of the province of Newfoundland. The village of Griquet, my own birthplace, is located near the northern tip of the Great Northern Peninsula, so its winters produced slightly milder, but similar, conditions to that of Labrador. So I have first-hand memories of the fierce January winds howling around the windows and doors of poorly insulated dwellings. In the barren landscape of Labrador those winds would be even more deadly. Yet Labrador became the destination of a number of Moravian missionaries. What motivated such abandon—such a high level of sacrifice? A study of revival history tells us that it was a life-transforming encounter with the

Christ of Calvary that caused them to leave the relative comfort and moderate climes of home to risk all in order to rescue souls. Those champions of the faith understood that the radical love of Christ, expressed through His death on the cross, required from them a radical commitment to the Lord and His cause.

I had the privilege of observing that same quality of extreme commitment a short while ago as I spoke with a career missionary who had spent much of her life serving in Afghanistan. She was still there as the coalition of nations combating terrorism moved into the country to unseat the Taliban-controlled state. The area, where she already faced hostility towards her work among Afghan women and children, suddenly became much more dangerous. Any Westerner remained in the country at great personal risk. Her agency recalled all of its missionaries from the region, which meant that she was required to exit to a safe haven at Pashawar in Pakistan. She told me how disappointed she was that she was asked to leave. She would have gladly stayed on in spite of the increased danger. In her mind there was no good reason to terminate her work. She had gone with the understanding that she was abandoning all for Christ, and the current increased danger factor made no difference to her. Christ's radical act of commitment to the will of the Father had set the bar for her. In light of Calvary, there was no sacrifice.

> Christ's work on the cross enables us to be united with Him, indwelt by Him, becoming all that we can be for His glory.

You and I may never have the opportunity to put our lives at risk for the cause of Christ. Yet Calvary's love exacts from us a level of devotion that says, in the words of an old hymn of consecration, "I'll go where You want me to go, dear Lord, o'er mountain or plain, or sea. I'll say what You want me to say, dear Lord. I'll be what You want me to be."[27] The song captures the thought that our willingness to **go** and **do** arises from our **being**. Christ's work on the cross enables us to be united with Him, indwelt by Him, becoming all that we can be for His glory.

That They May Be One

In spite of the many positives of my upbringing, I was very aware of denominational posturing and infighting within the Christian community. Other Christian faith traditions were often regarded as the enemy. Christians were polarized around the Salvation Army, Pentecostal, Brethren, United Church, or Anglican banner, and there was little or no collaboration among them. Furthermore, there were also significant challenges to true Biblical unity on the inside of those various church groups. Infighting and backbiting were not uncommon and served to weaken the testimony of the churches within their respective communities. From time to time, factions, divisions, and personal animosities would be challenged by a fresh work of the Holy Spirit. The result would be what was known as a "love feast," in which faults and injustices would be confessed and made right as the people of God would lay down their weapons and be reconciled to one another. These were times of rich spiritual blessing as pride and malice gave way to humility and genuine mutual submission and care. In the ebb and flow of "times of refreshing," the Lord did His greatest works in the lives of His people in an atmosphere of love and harmony.

Since growing in my understanding of the Scriptures, I see how inextricably tied into God's working and blessing in His Church—the vertical relationship—is the horizontal relationships among His people. Jesus' prayer to the Father in John chapter 17 accentuates the priority that God gives to how we relate to one another.

> *"I have given them the glory that you gave me, that they may be one as we are one: I in them and you in me. May they be brought to complete unity to let the world know that you sent me and have loved them even as you have loved me"* (John 17:22,23).

The impact the cross must have in our lives is not just one-dimensional (our relationship with God) but two-dimensional (our relationship with God and with one another). The apostle John wrote: *"We proclaim to you what we have seen and heard, so that you also may have fellowship with us. And our fellowship is with the Father and with his Son, Jesus Christ"* (1 John 1:3). Our fellowship with the Lord never precludes the need for fellowship with other believers but, instead, mandates it! The work of the cross was intended to remove, through the power of the blood, the barrier of sin that separated us from God. It also was targeting the barriers that exist among people. For example, *"the wall of partition"* that for centuries

115

had separated Jew from Gentile, Paul informs the church at Ephesus, was demolished by the blood of the cross (Ephesians 2:11–22 KJV). When we harbour resentment, when we choose to reject our brothers and sisters because of denominational stripes or ethnic differences, when we allow ill-conceived prejudices to distance us from those we should embrace, we deny the unifying effect the cross of Jesus should have upon our lives.

On the subject of denominational differences it excites me to see that the Church of today offers a good news story. As I travel across North America, and likewise to international destinations, I see an openness and acceptance among evangelical believers of differing doctrinal camps that was simply not there a generation ago. Worship styles and a general recognition of the commonality of our mission are causing denominational lines to be increasingly blurred. Certainly on the surface it's not normally easy to tell the difference between Baptists and Pentecostals or Mennonite and Christian and Missionary Alliance churches. An observation and a question: It's the Holy Spirit who brings unity. Could the Spirit of God be preparing His Church for another massive outpouring of His Spirit? Could it be that a spirit of unity among God's people could trigger an unprecedented outpouring of His Holy Spirit in the Church in our time?

> It's the Holy Spirit who brings unity. Could the Spirit of God be preparing His Church for another massive outpouring of His Spirit?

A picture of the connection of the Holy Spirit's outpouring and unity among believers is given to us in Psalm 133:

How good and pleasant it is when brothers live together in unity! It is like precious oil poured on the head, running down on the beard, running down on Aaron's beard, down upon the collar of his robes. It is as if the dew of Hermon were falling on Mount Zion. For there the LORD bestows his blessing, even life forevermore.

Surely, since Christ so strongly emphasized unity in His prayer to the Father (John 17), it must grieve the heart of God to view intolerance and disunity among His children. Conversely, where our unity wrought by Christ's redemptive work is recognized and celebrated, is He not ready and anxious to pour out the anointing of His Spirit to overflowing?

From the "low-level" perspective of human pride, selfish ambition, and historical separation, there is little hope for such reformation. Mount Calvary, the mountain of sacrifice, offers a different perspective, however. The love of Christ that compelled Him to lay down His life for us can both inspire and enable us to lay down our prejudices and self-interest and embrace one another. The greatest apologetic we can present to a cynical world is an unwavering, discernable love among the family of believers!

Earlier in this chapter we highlighted the grand theme of Calvary's cross: the substitutionary nature of Christ's death. The depth of His love for me—that He would take the penalty for my sin—seizes my attention and captures my heart. One of the cherished blessings resulting from my association with The Peoples Church in Toronto is to have become acquainted with the Scottish preacher, author, and statesman Dr. John Moore. John, who wrote the well-known song "Burdens Are Lifted At Calvary," brings a proper focus in his preaching and his writings on the redemptive work of Christ. Another song of his expresses the penetrating question "Why?"

Why did they nail Him to Calvary's tree?
Why? Tell me, why was He there?
Jesus the helper, the healer, the friend,
Why? Tell me, why was He there?

Chorus
All my iniquities on Him were laid,
He nailed them all to the tree.
Jesus, the debt of my sin fully paid,
He paid the ransom for me.

Why should He love me, a sinner undone?
Why? Tell me, why should He care?
I do not merit the love He has shown,
Why? Tell me why should He care?

Why should I linger afar from His love?
Why? Tell me, why should I fear?
Somehow I know I should venture, and prove;
Why? Tell me, why should I fear?"[28]

"Outside"

As I wrap up this chapter let me address an aspect of the Calvary experience that always challenges me and, in reality, defies human understanding, running totally counter to the human psyche. I speak of Christ's willingness to face—though so completely undeserving—scorn, misunderstanding, and humiliation without self-vindication. When I'm unjustly judged, when I'm ridiculed without reason, there's something within me that compels me to want to set the record straight. Jesus, on the other hand, allowed Himself to be shamed and vilified to the point of being cast out of the city, not deemed worthy to die within the city walls! The writer of the book of Hebrews speaks directly to the depth and horror of the shame He bore.

> *The high priest carries the blood of animals into the Most Holy Place as a sin offering, but the bodies are burned outside the camp. And so Jesus also suffered outside the city gate to make the people holy through his own blood. Let us, then, go to him outside the camp, bearing the disgrace he bore* (Hebrews 13:11–13).

The fact that He was crucified and buried outside the city adds particular weight to the rejection He suffered. Let's look at this in the Old Testament context. In Exodus 29:14 a bull is slain as a sin offering: *"Burn the bull's flesh and its hide and its offal outside the camp. It is a sin offering."* The body had to be treated as waste and burned outside the camp. It was a sin offering. Spiritually it speaks of the fact that Christ became sin for us: *"God made him who had no sin to be sin for us, so*

119

that in him we might become the righteousness of God" (2 Corinthians 5:21). It meant that He must be put to death outside the city. The apostle John describes the event. *"Carrying his own cross, he went out to the place of the Skull (which in Aramaic is called Golgotha). Here they crucified him"* (John 19:17,18). This actually was a literal fulfilment of the Old Testament symbol.

Here is what we need to understand: Just as the body parts of the bull, the sin offering, were put to the heat of the fire outside the camp, so the sin that Jesus bore caused Him to suffer the heat of God's justice outside the gate of the city. It signifies in a marked way the horror of the sin He bore, emphasizing to us the notion that sin must be discarded. The defilement of sin must not remain inside the place of God's presence. That's the situation as we see Him carrying His cross outside the city gate—not worthy to die or to be buried inside the city walls.

But the scene says more to us than that. In real terms it speaks of how totally Christ suffered rejection by the first-century world. The crucifixion meant that He was rejected from Roman society. K. W. Osbeck writes, "Death by crucifiction was one of the worst forms of dying. No Roman citizen was ever crucified."[25] It was reserved for outcasts. He was rejected by Jewish society. Jewish law stated, *"Cursed is everyone who is hung on a tree"* (Galatians 3:13). He was rejected by the city of Jerusalem as its leaders and citizens cried, *"Away with Him! Crucify Him!"* (John 19:15 NKJV).

He was cast out by every sector and every level of Jerusalem society. The business sector had no place for the one who exposed their corrupt practices and their deceit. The social sector accused Him of dubious alliances, suggesting He spent too much time with sinners. No self-respecting teacher would spend time with the Zacchaeuses and the Mary Magdalenes of the world. The political sector had no tolerance for the one who insisted on honest leadership—who Himself made claims of divine authority. The religious sector had no patience for the one who exposed them for the hypocrites that they were. They were the ones who actually initiated the assault on His person. The rich were intolerant of His teachings *"Do not lay up for yourselves treasures on earth"* (Matthew 6:19 NKJV) and *"Seek first the kingdom of God"* (Matthew 6:33 NKJV). Finally, on Mount Calvary He was even rejected by many of the poor, for He was no longer in a place to feed them and address their needs. Viewing Him as "down and out," everyone joined forces and together kicked Him out—right outside the city.

In our twenty-first-century smugness we gasp at the cruel and barbaric actions of those first-century rogues! But let's look again. He is still rejected by the business sector of today. There's still no place for the one who insists on absolute moral and ethical standards of conduct. There's still no place for the display of concern and prioritized treatment for the poor and those who are exploited. That's just not good business practice. He is still rejected by the social sector. It's absurd to love our neighbour as ourselves and to think of others as better than ourselves. His teaching on individual responsibility still doesn't fly. The religious sector of today determine Him to be too narrow in His thinking—much too intolerant. The educational sector finds Him too controversial. They take careful steps to avoid even the mention of His name, even at Christmastime! The political sector of today find Him too direct and dogmatic in His views and too politically incorrect. Yes, His name and His cross still bring reproach to the enlightened society of the twenty-first century. In fact, the most convenient place for Jesus Christ is "outside."

> Yes, His name and His cross still bring reproach to the enlightened society of the twenty-first century. In fact, the most convenient place for Jesus Christ is "outside."

So the question we must reckon with as we look squarely at the implications of what took place on Mount Calvary is this: "Are we willing to face the same kind of rejection for His name's sake?" My observation, as I look at today's evangelical churches, is that we are in a constant struggle for acceptance within the broader culture. We soften our message, we use doublespeak, and we adopt the norms of the dominant culture—all driven by a perceived need to be "relevant." I have the feeling that the Church fears rejection by society more than it has at any other time in Church history. We need to be reawakened to the words of Jesus *"Blessed are you when men hate you, when they exclude you and insult you and reject your name as evil, because of the Son of Man"* (Luke 6:22). He bore complete vilification and was totally ostracized from the same world we continually vie for acceptance in! As the writer to the Hebrews exhorts, *"Let us, then, go to him outside the camp, bearing the disgrace he bore"*

(Hebrews 13:13). Can the Church of today bear the stigma of being stereotyped and marginalized by popular culture? It seems that a willingness to identify truly with the Christ of Calvary is bound to take us there.

Yes, Mount Calvary mandates a return to the notion of sacrifice.

> Were the whole realm of nature mine;
> That were a present far too small.
> Love so amazing, so divine,
> Demands my soul, my life, my all.[30]

In reflecting on this central message of the Christian faith, would you join me in this prayer?

Dear Lord Jesus, I am so inclined to take Your love, so wonderfully expressed for me at Calvary, for granted. I can't begin to enter into the degree of physical and emotional suffering You endured. You took no shortcuts and spared Yourself no pain to redeem my soul.

Forgive me for so readily accepting Your cleansing while, at the same time, being so unwilling to give of myself for You. Let me see clearly my need to identify with Your death so that I might experience the fullness of Your resurrection life. Teach me to be willing to bear reproach for Your name's sake. May I daily make decisions, tough decisions, that will display that I prefer to honour You in all I do.

May Your Church distinguish itself from the world by fully identifying with the disgrace and rejection You bore on Mount Calvary. May we all be willing to go with You to Mount Calvary and identify with Your death and suffering, and may we be willing to make sacrifices for the greatest cause—the cause of Your cross.

Amen.

EIGHT

Mount Zion:
The Mountain of His Presence

Many nations will come and say, "Come, let us go up to the mountain of the LORD, to the house of the God of Jacob. He will teach us his ways, so that we may walk in his paths." The law will go out from Zion, the word of the LORD from Jerusalem
(Micah 4:2).

For the LORD has chosen Zion, he has desired it for his dwelling
(Psalm 132:13).

A VIVID MEMORY FROM MY PRIMARY-SCHOOL DAYS IS A VISIT to my classroom by a police officer. We rarely had visits from the "Mounties" (Royal Canadian Mounted Police) in our community. We were, however, fully aware of the existence of the police and held a reverential fear of them. We lived in an orderly and, for the most part, peaceful world, always aware of the reach of the "long arm of the law." From my perspective as a young boy, I viewed the police as the full embodiment of the law and was naturally quite enthralled by the power of a policeman. Now here he was, larger than life in his official red-jacketed uniform, worn for official public functions. The bright red jacket, the black trousers sporting the broad yellow stripe on each leg, and the high leather boots all added to the austerity of the policeman's presence. I could hardly believe that an officer could be speaking to us from the front of the

classroom! I, like all of my classmates, was awed, fasci-
nated, and overwhelmed by the experience. Any misbe-
haviour, even by the most rowdy among us, was incon-
ceivable. It's one thing to have a police presence in one's
region. It's quite another thing to hear the thunderous
clap of an officer's footsteps on the hardwood floor of
one's classroom! I know the illustration is weak, but it
does help us understand that there is a difference
between having our lives influenced by the message
and the reality of Christianity and experiencing the
immediate and empowering presence of God.

We discussed in chapter 4 the remarkable thought
that we will one day be where the Lord is. The
thought is astounding that we will be able to perceive
and interact with our Creator with real, immediate,
full-sensory awareness. The Bible identifies the place
of His dwelling as Mount Zion. Here are some of the
Old Testament Scriptures that speak about Zion as the
abode of God:

> *"I have installed my King on Zion, my holy hill"*
> (Psalm 2:6).
> *Sing praises to the Lord, enthroned in Zion; proclaim
> among the nations what he has done* (Psalm 9:11).
> *From Zion, perfect in beauty, God shines forth*
> (Psalm 50:2).
> *May the LORD, the Maker of heaven and earth,
> bless you from Zion* (Psalm 134:3).
> *We are signs and symbols in Israel from the LORD
> Almighty, who dwells on Mount Zion* (Isaiah 8:18).

I think that deep down inside of every believer in
Christ is the desire to experience His presence in a

richer, deeper, and fuller dimension. What I want to address here is something that is not easily defined—the glory of the Lord's presence experienced in a way that is different from the normative day-to-day involvement of the Spirit in and through the life of the believer. There's a verse in the

> It is possible to experience the presence of God in a dimension that is special, whereby He "draws close" to us.

book of James that makes a simple but compelling statement: *"Draw near to God and He will draw near to you"* (James 4:8 NKJV). Just think about the implications of this promise: God has given us the opportunity to get close to Him! It is possible to experience the presence of God in a dimension that is special, whereby He "draws close" to us. I'm referring to the possibility of experiencing God in a manner perhaps not generally realized by many in our generation.

There have been times—times we know of in recent Church history—when the Lord has visited His Church with a display of His presence that is extraordinary and indescribable. Colin H. Peckham tells of an unusual outpouring of God's Spirit in the northwest islands (the Hebrides) off the coast of Scotland in the early 1950s:

> Between the years 1949 and 1953 the Spirit of God was poured out in a most remarkable way on the Isle-of-Lewis in the Western Isles of Scotland. The instrument God used in this movement was Rev. Duncan Campbell...This revival was known in many parts of the world as "The Lewis Awakening," and its news has been the means of stirring Christians everywhere

to pray that God would again visit His people in great power and blessing.[31]

In pursuing this topic, I spoke with my friend Dr. John Moore and asked him if he knew of the atmosphere purported to have existed during the Hebrides Revival in coastal Scotland. John was pastor of the great Tent Hall in Glasgow, Scotland, in the early fifties. To my surprise John said to me in his strong Scottish brogue, "I was tharr."

Evidently Duncan Campbell himself, whom God used strategically in the awakening, urged John to force himself away from the demands of his pastoral duties at Tent Hall to go to Lewis, the centre of the outpouring. "John, you must go," said Campbell.

What John observed as he visited the region was a dynamic visitation of God's presence upon the community. He said to me, "Reg, it was powerful. People in the community were gripped by God's presence. One man was plowing his field. So moved was he by his need for forgiveness that he stopped his tractor and fell to the ground in repentance."

Duncan Campbell gives a first-hand commentary on the event:

> In revival, God moves in the district. Suddenly, the community becomes God conscious. The Spirit of God grips men and women in such a way that even work is given up as people give themselves to waiting upon God. In the midst of the Lewis Awakening, the parish minister at Barvas wrote, "The Spirit of the Lord was resting wonderfully on the different townships of the region. His Presence was in the homes of

the people, on meadow and moorland, and even on the public roads."

This presence of God is the supreme characteristic of a God-sent revival. Of the hundreds who found Jesus Christ during this time fully seventy-five percent were saved before they came near a meeting or heard a sermon by myself or any other ministers in the parish. The power of God, the Spirit of God, was moving in operation, and the fear of God gripped the souls of men—this is God-sent revival as distinct from special efforts in the field of evangelism.[32]

Speaking of the surprising move of God in the community of Barvas, Campbell reported the following:

They had arranged for me to address the church at a short meeting beginning at nine o'clock that night. It was a remarkable meeting. God sovereignly moved, and there was an awareness of God which was wonderful. The meeting lasted until four o'clock in the morning, and I had not witnessed anything to compare with it at any other time during my ministry.

Around midnight, a group of young people left a dance and crowded into the church. There were people who couldn't go to sleep because they were so gripped by God. Although there was an awareness of God and a spirit of conviction at this initial meeting, the real breakthrough came a few days later on Sunday night in the parish church.

The church was full, and the Spirit of God was moving in such a way that I couldn't preach. I just stood still and gazed upon the wondrous moving of God. Men and women were crying out to God for mercy all over the church. There was no appeal made whatsoever. After meeting for over three hours, I pronounced the benediction and told the people to go out, but mentioned that any who wanted to continue the meeting could come back later. A young deacon came to me and said, "Mr. Campbell, God is hovering over us."[33]

All who gave first-hand accounts of the event attested to the indefinable, yet real, powerful presence of God. Another eye-witness report gave the following review:

What had happened in Barvas was repeated over and over again. The sacred presence of God was everywhere. Sinners found themselves unable to escape it. Before the revival, Stornoway had one of the highest drinking rates in Scotland, and "bothans," illegal and unlicensed drinking places, flourished. After the revival, one publican mourned, "The drink trade on the Island is ruined."[34]

The author of this particular Web site article quotes Duncan Campbell as he gives an informed response to the phenomenon:

"Those who seek God for revival must be prepared for God to work in His own way and not according to their programme. His sovereignty does not relieve men of responsibility. God is the God of revival, but man is the human agent through whom revival is possible. Desire for revival is one thing, confident anticipation that their desire will be fulfilled is another."[35]

As we consider Campbell's observations, the obvious question is foisted upon us: "Are we, the Church of today, prepared for God to work in His own way in bringing revival to His people?" Are we ready to pray that by His sovereign will He will once again move within His people and manifest His presence in a manner that will transform not only the Church but the broader community as well?

In the book of 1 Kings, Solomon had completed the building of the temple and offered a powerful prayer of petition to God. The Lord responded with a promise that has become perhaps the most quoted Bible reference as an encouragement to pray:

"If my people, who are called by my name, will humble themselves and pray and seek my face and turn from their wicked ways, then will I hear from heaven and will forgive their sin and will heal their land" (2 Chronicles 7:14).

Prior to this the Lord had given a rare display of His glory. There was an overwhelming demonstration of God's presence, the glory of the Lord filling the temple so that the priests could not stand to minister: *"The priests could not perform their service because of the cloud, for the glory of the LORD filled the temple of God"* (2 Chronicles 5:14). That's what I mean—the Lord showing up in a way that is extraordinary and compelling.

Do you...do I...does the Church of today hold a deep longing to experience such a display of God's glory? I cannot begin to speculate where the majority of believers are when it comes to desire for true revival—a true demonstration of God's presence. I choose to believe that, given the need for "house repair" that has been highlighted in this work, there exists at least a hint of desire to see a dramatic visitation of God to our Church—our nation.

> Do you...do I...does the Church of today hold a deep longing to experience such a display of God's glory?

Such a demonstration of God's presence is life-transforming to those who become recipients of its power.

Moses' Emphatic Request

It was not unusual for Moses to have intimate communion with God. His "burning bush" experience and his Mt. Sinai experiences reveal a level of intimate communication that is unparalleled in Scripture. Yet, in spite of these encounters—or perhaps because of these encounters—Moses possessed a deep desire to, first of all, have the manifest presence of God among the Israelites and, secondly, to experience God's glory. Moses, as we saw in chapter 3, essentially tells the Lord that if His evidential presence does not accompany them, there is no point in moving forward. Then he takes it a step further and asks if he can observe the Lord's glory. Moses possessed a desperate need—a hunger to experience God in a deep and personal way.

> *Then Moses said to him, "If your Presence does not go with us, do not send us up from here. How will anyone know that you are pleased with me and with your people unless you go with us? What else will*

distinguish me and your people from all the other people on the face of the earth?" And the LORD said to Moses, "I will do the very thing you have asked, because I am pleased with you and I know you by name." Then Moses said, "Now show me your glory" (Exodus 33:15–18).

What follows are the self-describing words of the Lord. They indicate to us that to see the Lord's glory is to grasp a clear understanding of His character (good, merciful, and compassionate) and that He is holy (distinct and set apart).

And the LORD said, "I will cause all my goodness to pass in front of you, and I will proclaim my name, the LORD, in your presence. I will have mercy on whom I will have mercy, and I will have compassion on whom I will have compassion. But," he said, "you cannot see my face, for no one may see me and live." Then the LORD said, "There is a place near me where you may stand on a rock. When my glory passes by, I will put you in a cleft in the rock and cover you with my hand until I have passed by. Then I will remove my hand and you will see my back; but my face must not be seen" (Exodus 33:19–23).

We noted earlier that the symbolism here is strongly prophetic. We may see the glory of the Lord as we stand on the Rock, Jesus Christ. His hand of mercy has been extended to cover our sins. Let's observe the Lord's fulfillment of Moses' request.

Then the LORD came down in the cloud and stood there with him and proclaimed his name, the LORD.

133

And he passed in front of Moses, proclaiming, "The LORD, the LORD, the compassionate and gracious God, slow to anger, abounding in love and faithfulness, maintaining love to thousands, and forgiving wickedness, rebellion and sin. Yet he does not leave the guilty unpunished" (Exodus 34:5–7).

The glory of God is seen in His Church as we look intently into the express image of His Person, the Lord Jesus Christ. To gain a vision of God's glory is to see the wonders of God embodied in Jesus Christ—His character, His goodness, His justice, and His mercy. The Holy Spirit, who bears witness to Christ (1 John 5:6–8), assures us that in every true revival the focus will be on Jesus. Isaiah's response to an up-close encounter with Christ in all His glory in Isaiah 6:5 is: *"Woe is me! for I am undone"* (KJV). A close encounter with God through the work of His Spirit will likewise make us acutely aware of our own "undoneness" and the holiness and the sufficiency of Christ. Whether or not you and I are privileged in our lifetime to experience the presence of God in the way that others have—like those who witnessed the Hebrides Revival—His faithfulness means that He already does declare His compassion, His love, and His justice to us daily. He is faithful! When the vessel He desires to use is open and available, He will show up in transforming, sanctifying power!

> To gain a vision of God's glory is to see the wonders of God embodied in Jesus Christ—His character, His goodness, His justice, and His mercy.

Draw Near

The Lord's ready response to the request of Moses reveals that He loves to interact with His people. In Old Testament times a ritualistic path had to be followed in order for the priest to access the Holy of Holies. First there was the ascent to the temple, followed by the entrance to the outer court where the sacrifice was offered. Then there was the ceremonial washing and the entrance into the inner court, or the Holy Place, where incense was offered before proceeding into the Holy of Holies. In Exodus 25 the Lord assures Moses that, once he had gone through the various stages and entered the Holy of Holies, He would meet with him between the wings of the cherubim. *"There, above the cover between the two cherubim that are over the ark of the Testimony, I will meet with you"* (Exodus 25:22). What a remarkable promise that is, the God of creation defining the conditions and the place where He will meet with His servant! When Jesus died, the veil separating the inner court from the Holy of Holies was ripped apart (Matthew 27:51), giving you and me access to the presence of God. Because of the blood of the eternal covenant, we may now meet with God directly.

> The Lord's ready response to the request of Moses reveals that He loves to interact with His people.

What a prospect! What an invitation! The writer to the Hebrews reminds us that because of the "new and living way" we may now draw near to God without ceremony or rite. He contrasts the circumstances of Moses' encounters with God and the way that we who know Christ may experience Him:

> *But you have come to Mount Zion, to the heavenly Jerusalem, the city of the living God. You have come to thousands upon thousands of angels in joyful assembly, to the church of the firstborn, whose names are written in heaven. You have come to God, the judge of all men, to the spirits of righteous men made perfect, to Jesus the mediator of a new covenant* (Hebrews 12:22–24).

Have you felt that you've been following the Lord from a distance, longing to know Him more deeply but always feeling that you are, or that He is, miles away? Take time. Through Jesus we may enter in. He will manifest Himself—His goodness, His loving-kindness, His character—to you in such a way that the material world begins to lose its lustre.

Before I see renewal in the Church, I must understand that it needs to first happen in me. May the Lord, by His sovereign grace, give us a renewed passion to experience the glory of His presence in a manner we haven't yet known. It is then that *"the glory of this present house,"* in Haggai's words, will show that it is demonstrably *"greater than the glory of the former house"* (Haggai 2:9). The prophet Ezekiel gives a detailed description of the rebuilt temple. When all is complete according to the specifications that the Lord had given, and the practice of worship restored, the prophet concludes with the statement *"And the name of the city from that time on will be: 'The LORD Is There'"* (Ezekiel 48:35).

A favourite song for us kids, maybe because of its upbeat tempo, concluded with these lines: "We're marching to Zion; beautiful, beautiful Zion. We're marching upward to Zion, the beautiful city of God."[36] Coming at the end of a service, after my dad had preached a rousing sermon on the beauties of heaven, the song stirred within me a whole range of pleasant thoughts—not all of them spiritual: The long service was finally about to end. A wonderful Sunday dinner (The midday meal was the main meal and we called it "dinner") was awaiting me at home. Oh, and heaven was going to be a cool place to end up. Not anywhere near my thoughts was the incredible truth that I may, in this life, experience the rich presence of the one whose dwelling place is called Zion. You and I are the new Zion, the place of His presence.

I believe the Lord desires to fill His house again with a fresh demonstration of His glory. If that's also your conviction, I ask you to join me in praying:

Dear Lord, I thank You that Your abiding presence has been the one constant in my life since the day I asked You to come into my heart. Just as Your Word has promised, You have never left me nor forsaken me (Hebrews 13:5). How I praise You for Your consistent care over my life, for answers to specific prayers, and even for times when darkness seemed to overtake me and it seemed that I had lost my way! Yet You have proven that You were at work through it all—for my good. I praise You because You are a faithful God.

Lord, I have heard of times when Your presence has been displayed in such a way that Your people have been renewed, Your Church enlivened, and society transformed. Surely, we today have as great a need for a new visitation of Your presence as at any time in Church history. Our moral drifting, our fractured families, our self-direction, and our pride speak to a need for the healing, restoring work of Your Spirit to be outpoured.

Lord, too often I hear that, even among the emerging generation, there is no sense of God's presence among the fellowship of believers. Experiencing a true God-encounter, even as Your Church worships and serves together, is rare or seemingly non-existent. Let the imprint of Your character—Your grace, Your goodness, Your love—be acutely experienced in Your house again.

"Lord, prepare me to be a sanctuary."[37] Come to this temple and display the awesomeness of Your glory. Purify my life and let me be a channel of Your truth, Your justice, and Your mercy. Let me progress from glory to glory (2 Corinthians 3:18 KJV) in the knowledge of Your truth and in the power of Your Spirit. Let others see the glory of Christ in me. And may society see the glory of Christ in a Church that is renewed and transformed.

Amen.

NINE

Following Christ to the Mountain of Prayer

Now it came to pass in those days that He went out to the mountain to pray, and continued all night in prayer to God
(Luke 6:12 NKJV).

I WAS STILL QUITE YOUNG WHEN I DISCOVERED THAT PRAYER could be hard work. It required dedication and focus. It was prayer meeting night, and for the first time I was allowed to join the older kids and the adults in the church in the weekly "calling on God." The format of the service went something like this: There would be a time of singing songs relating to the subject of prayer, like "Sweet Hour of Prayer," "For You I Am Praying," and "Revive Us Again." After a brief teaching from the Word of God, everyone would find a place at the front of the church auditorium to kneel and spend the next hour in prayer. One would voice an enthusiastic prayer amidst the phrases of agreement from among the entire group, then another, and then another. After an extended time of audible prayer, one by one the participants would go back to their original seats. There was an understanding that the prayer meeting was not considered over until the last person had gotten up from his knees and returned to his seat.

I was the last one on my knees. The folks waited and waited, but I remained in apparent deep intercession. Eventually my mom, who knew that I lacked the spiritual depth to remain praying for that long, came and tapped me on the shoulder. I had been sound asleep! It would be a while before I would be ready to tackle the prayer meeting again.

So corporate prayer was a normal part of the spiritual walk of believers. In my parents' tradition, prayer was understood to be a necessary function—a necessary preoccupation of the church if the church was to see the transforming work of the Holy Spirit reviving God's people and impacting society. They knew of the role of prayer in the much talked about outpourings earlier in the century. They knew that the Welsh Revival, the Azusa Street Revival, the renewal in western Canada in the 1940s, and the revival in the Hebrides had all followed a time of concerted prayer on the part of the people of God. So prayer was seen to be a means by which God uses His people to bring about demonstrations of His goodness and grace. One's commitment to prayer seemed to be regarded as the true test of spiritual maturity and depth.

But has the formal "going through the motions" of prayer left us with an inadequate view of its purpose and nature? To gain a proper perspective on prayer it's always useful to observe how Jesus approached the question.

Jesus Models Prayer

While there was something very positive about the consistent practice of prayer in my tradition, there was at times a seeming desperation in the approach. My understanding of prayer as being a normal function in the life of the believer was greatly influenced by my mother, in addition to, but in contrast with, the public practices of prayer. Mom prayed regularly, spending protracted periods in the Lord's presence. She petitioned the Lord for protection and provision for her family, but there was more to it than completing a checklist of needs. What made prayer a joy for my mom was relationship. This, I believe, is a key to the rediscovery of prayer in today's Church. It is much more about being confident of one's relationship with God than about attempting to get God's attention to satisfy one's list of wants (be they material or spiritual). So, there it is again—a theme that has surfaced in every chapter of this book—what is needed to build obedience, truth, hope, and faith in today's Church (in your life and mine) is a renewal of relationship with the Lord.

> It seems to me that this was the primary motivation for His rich prayer life—His relationship with the Father.

Time after time during Jesus' earthly ministry He withdrew from the crowds, and even from the disciples, to be alone with the Father. It seems to me that this was the primary motivation for His rich prayer life—His relationship with the Father. As a matter of fact, He gives us that message rather directly. In the religious tradition of the first-century culture it was customary to pray in public to draw attention to oneself. Jesus used that as a foil to genuine relational praying.

"And when you pray, do not be like the hypocrites, for they love to pray standing in the synagogues and on the street corners to be seen by men. I tell you the truth, they have received their reward in full. But when you pray, go into your room, close the door and pray to your Father, who is unseen. Then your Father, who sees what is done in secret, will reward you" (Matthew 6:5,6).

Jesus' well known high-priestly prayer in John 17 is a vivid illustration of how prayer for Him was an expression of intimacy. While it is an example of deep intercession, it is also a place where He speaks of the special relationship He has with the Father. *"I have brought you glory on earth by completing the work you gave me to do. And now, Father, glorify me in your presence with the glory I had with you before the world began"* (John 17:4,5). The close personal relationship between Jesus and the Father is further underlined as we read on in the chapter:

"Father, I want those you have given me to be with me where I am, and to see my glory, the glory you have given me because you loved me before the creation of the world. Righteous Father, though the world does not know you, I know you, and they know that you have sent me. I have made you known to them, and will continue to make you known in order that the love you have for me may be in them and that I myself may be in them" (John 17:24–26).

The Place of Prayer Today

As I write this I'm making my way home via public transit (I don't write while I'm driving!) from a regular Wednesday night prayer meeting at The Peoples Church, Toronto. The attendees—mostly seniors—together form about 1 percent of our Sunday attendance. Good, faithful people, they have, for the most part, been attending mid-week prayer for a number of decades now. They believe in the value of prayer but, certainly from the perspective of sheer numbers, could hardly be considered a strong force for change. This is not dissimilar to the majority of churches in North America today. An emphasis on prayer seems to be a sure way to shoo people away from a gathering. Prayer is still acknowledged as being important. Books are still written on the subject. The unfortunate fact is that there seems to be an absence of a sustained practice of prayer in the churches.

How do we address this need? To try to shame believers into support of prayer would simply be counterproductive. We need a renewed appreciation for the value of prayer initiated by our sovereign Lord. In the Hebrides Revival the Lord put it in the hearts of two senior sisters to devote themselves to seek God for a spiritual renewal in their region. Likewise, as already mentioned, from the perspective of revival history it seems that God first involves His people by calling them to prayer before pouring out His blessing in revival fire. Dr. Thomas Miller, a Canadian author and teacher, wrote in the mid 1980s a book titled *Ripe for Revival: The Churches at the Crossroads of Renewal or Decline*. Based on an in-depth study of revival history, Miller has this to say:

The potential for renewal is dependent on the divinely-sanctioned methods of the past—prayer, preaching and the providence of God. Every great renewal movement has been initiated and carried on by intercessory prayer, fervent preaching and total dependence on the divine providence.[38]

Of the three criteria identified by Miller, there is only one that most of us have any control over. That function is intercessory prayer. (The objects of our praying well ought to be the other two—fervent, Biblical preaching and the moving of God's hand of blessing.)

But, you may well argue, in the fast-paced lives we live in the Western world, how can we add intercessory prayer to an already full agenda? Without trying to be cynical, the obvious question comes to mind: "Whose agenda are we following?" Henry Blackaby, in his widely read book *Experiencing God*, very clearly advances the idea that God is at work in reconciling the world unto Himself. We have an obligation to find out what God is doing and accept His direction to join in.

God takes the initiative to involve His people with Him in His work. He does this on His timetable, not on ours. He is the One who is already at work in our world. When He opens your spiritual eyes to see where He is at work, that revelation is your invitation to join Him...When God reveals His work to you, that is the time He wants you to begin adjusting to Him and His activity.[39]

How do we develop an astuteness for determining what God is doing? I believe the answer is by maintaining a vital personal relationship with Him. In our private quiet times before God, in our small-group meetings, in our church services and other venues, let's become more open to communication with the Lord—not through constructing long and eloquent cliché-filled prayers but through simple heart-to-heart communion. That's the way my relationship with Him can be built and strengthened. The result will be a new synergy between our yielded lives and the Holy Spirit of God. Let's be open, connected vessels! The Holy Spirit desires to pray for us and through us. It is that divine connection that results in the accomplishment of His purposes.

> The Holy Spirit desires to pray for us and through us. It is that divine connection that results in the accomplishment of His purposes.

I remember hearing my parents speak of times when there was a dramatic sense of God's Spirit at work in a community simply as a result of God's people being tuned in to the working of His Holy Spirit. It is not something that is formulaic or theologically complex. It grows out of the dramatic interaction of God among His people. When we allow our faith to grow and believe that God is at work, our obedience becomes vitally linked to His activity. In his recent book *Connect with the Heart of God,* Charles Price points out that God wants more than a passive dependence on Him.

God delivers through our obedience; every act of God in the history of Israel is precipitated by an act of obedience. We don't sit back, arms folded, "God, you do it, I'm watching. Save my neighbours, please." No, go and talk to your neighbours, in dependency on God. You act in obedience.[40]

What's your level of hunger for something new and fresh from God? Do you long to see the darkness lifted from the minds of our countrymen as the glory of the Lord is displayed among His people? Let's come to God with a renewed appreciation for the simplicity of Biblical faith. We serve a merciful God who is *"not wanting anyone to perish, but everyone to come to repentance"* (2 Peter 3:9). Let's discover what it means to rest in His finished work and believe that He desires to build His Church and impact our society through us. So, when I speak of praying, I am not advocating desperate pleading but a level of communication and communion with God that is solidly rooted in a strong and vibrant relationship with Him. Let's combine faith with action and see what powerful ways God will work in us to bring hope, cleansing, and transformation to our neighbourhoods, our nation, and our world!

The prophet Habakkuk was used of the Lord to identify the reality of God's kingdom work among His people in the past and made a specific request that God demonstrate His power once again *"in our time."* *"LORD, I have heard of your fame; I stand in awe of your deeds, O LORD. Renew them in our day, in our time make them known; in wrath remember mercy"* (Habakkuk 3:2).

Who knows but that God may be preparing us to once again manifest His glory in dramatic measure in our day? Yes, I said "preparing us." The amazing and dynamic truth is that in the present Church Age God has chosen to do His work and manifest His character and His salvation through His Church. He does

> Who knows but that God may be preparing us to once again manifest His glory in dramatic measure in our day?

not carry on His work of redemption—of building His Church—independent of His Church. His Church is the temple of the Holy Spirit. That means you and me! *"Do you not know that your body is a temple of the Holy Spirit, who is in you, whom you have received from God? You are not your own"* (1 Corinthians 6:19). It's important as we remember that we are the habitation of the Holy Spirit that we also recall that Jesus said, *"My house will be called a house of prayer for all nations"* (Mark 11:17). Let's not be found guilty of "quenching" the Holy Spirit by filling our lives with earthly, temporal pursuits and not being cognizant of His work and His direction in our lives. Let's instead offer our lives—His house—as a place where prayer is given priority.

Do you see how vitally linked we are to the purpose and work of God in the earth? That, fundamentally, is why this book has been written—to emphasize the need for "repair" in a number of areas where today's Church has become weak. Will you take it as your responsibility to see that the values of obedience, truth, hope, faith, revelation, sacrifice, and a desire for the fullness of His presence are restored to His temple? Let's make the following prayer a first step up that mountain.

Dear Lord, You have modeled prayer as an expression of relationship with the Father. Can it be that the disinclination to pray on the part of today's Church is a reflection of a weakened relationship with You? Is the will and purpose of God being thwarted in our generation through a lack of connectedness with the God of restoration and renewal? Are You at this hour calling us back to the simplicity of relationship as opposed to the complexity of form and methodology?

O Creator and Restorer of all things, give us eyes that see the spiritual barrenness of the Church in our times. Give us a hunger for Your righteousness in our own lives. Give us a passion for the redeeming work of the cross to be effected in our lives, in the Church, and in society.

Come indwell us in Your fullness. Let the glory of Your presence cause us to stand out in our thinking, our conduct, our joy, and our approach to life. But amidst the joy that we experience in Your presence, let there grow in us a genuine passion for souls. Let us see Your world as You see it. Give us a renewed awareness that outside of Your redeeming grace the world is lost and condemned. Let the fountain of grace that was opened "for sin and for all uncleanness" flow freely in our lives.

Let, O Lord, the redeeming, transforming love of Christ be evident throughout Your

Church. Then let it overflow from Your Church into every stratum of society. May our educational systems, our social initiatives, and our public policy be dramatically influenced by the radiant splendour of Your grace and mercy emanating from a Church that is filled with Your glory.

We fervently pray the prayer of Your servant Habakkuk: *"LORD, I have heard of your fame; I stand in awe of your deeds, O LORD. Renew them in our day, in our time make them known; in wrath remember mercy"* (Habakkuk 3:2).

Amen.

TEN

The Mountain of Commission

Then the eleven disciples went to Galilee, to the mountain where Jesus had told them to go...Then Jesus came to them and said, "All authority in heaven and on earth has been given to me. Therefore go and make disciples of all nations, baptizing them in the name of the Father and of the Son and of the Holy Spirit, and teaching them to obey everything I have commanded you. And surely I am with you always, to the very end of the age"
(Matthew 28:16–20).

A POSITIVE ASPECT OF MY TRADITION OF FAITH WAS THE built-in expectancy of a better tomorrow. "God will fulfill His promises." "God will lead us into greener pastures." "God will bring great blessing to my life." "God will send revival." "God will bring home the lost." This approach engendered hope and trust, but it also had the potential to leave us in a "wait until tomorrow" mode of thinking. I believe the enemy has used this ploy against the Church, generally with considerable success. "We'll see God move in the way that we desire when revival comes." "We'll see the lost come to Christ by the thousands when revival comes." "Our families and neighbours will be saved when revival comes."

What should our posture be as we await the renewing, reviving moving of the hand of God? In my conversations with the great churchman Dr. John Moore, he shared with me a perspective that was driven home to him as he interacted with the saints God used during His visitation to the Hebrides. "There are seasons," said John, "when by an act of His sovereign will, God visits His Church in an unusual display of His presence." John's conviction is that this is not something we can orchestrate. Our obligation is to be sensitive and obedient to His voice. Be ready and willing to pray as He calls us to pray. Be ready and willing to respond to the promptings of His Holy Spirit.

John had the remarkable privilege of conversing with the elderly sisters the Lord used as catalysts for the outpouring of His Spirit in the town of Lewis. One informed him that after a season of prayer the Lord gave her the assurance that He was about to visit the church in revival fire. She, in obedience to the Lord's leading, pulled on her shawl one evening, went to the parson's house, and informed him that God was going to visit the local church in an unusual and powerful outpouring. The minister received her word gladly and joined her in expectancy. Duncan Campbell was one of the guest speakers at a church leaders' conference in Ireland when the Lord gave him the strange message that he, though a scheduled speaker, must leave the conference and go immediately to Lewis. God was getting His people ready for an incredible demonstration of His convicting, redeeming love in the community of Lewis and the Hebrides Islands. God "showed up," bringing heart-breaking conviction to saints and sinners and radically impacting the region for His glory. How amazing this must have been! Do you long for a similar visitation of the presence of the Almighty? If you've stayed with me throughout this book, the answer is likely an unqualified "Yes."

But what should our posture be as we wait for a similar work of God's grace? That we need such a visitation in our time is without dispute. There's a simple verse in Paul's instruction to the church in Corinth, *"It is required in stewards that one be found faithful"* (1 Corinthians 4:2 NKJV). One revivalist has said, "While awaiting revival, carry on the work."

"Go Make Disciples"

Jesus' words to His disciples at that final mountaintop encounter have reverberated throughout the Church for centuries. Because the Church has generally responded with obedience, millions have been rescued and brought into the kingdom. The People Church in Toronto has a great tradition of global consciousness engendered by the passionate vision of the founder, Oswald J. Smith. He wrote:

> Our statement declares that we stand pre-eminently for the conversion of souls, the edification of believers and world-wide evangelism. There is nothing in that but what appears on the surface. We are old-fashioned, for we still believe in "the conversion of souls." Men need salvation. This neglected truth must be emphasized as never before...And our evangelism is by no means confined to our own city. Thank God, it is worldwide.[41]

This passion took Smith to multiple destinations around the globe, and we continue to receive first-hand reports from many parts of the world of those whose lives were radically altered by his life and teachings.

So our calling is to continue this great project—this

Missio Dei (Mission of God)—in our generation. The Church cannot *sit and wait*. We must rather *stand and go!* The enemies of the cross continue on many fronts to try to discredit the claims of our Lord and the authenticity of the Scriptures. You've heard it said that in any combat the best defence is a good offence. The gates of hell shall not prevail against the Church (see Matthew 16:18). May you and I become mobilized to find where and how God by His Spirit is at work. The operative term here is *mobilized*. If we feed the hungry, give help to the disenfranchised, minister hope to the distressed—more particularly, work with the inner-city poor, reach out and give a helping hand to the many refugees in our cities, assist the single mom who may be just a stone's throw away, or obey God's voice to carry His divine life to the throw-away kids of Calcutta's teeming streets—we will find the Lord's strength and grace powerfully at work within us. We will thereby position the Church for great victories—victories that will multiply as the Lord fills our lives afresh with His holy presence.

> The Church cannot *sit and wait*. We must rather *stand and go!*

"Teaching Them Everything…"

It's easy to get caught up in the big idea conveyed in the Great Commission. *"All the world,"* *"preach the gospel"* (Mark 16:15 NKJV), and *"baptizing them"* (Matthew 28:19) are phrases that excited me in my growing-up years about the prospect of spiritual conquests. This has also been the rallying cry of the

Church generally. We have often de-emphasized the equally great responsibility, contained in Jesus' command, of teaching. Teaching involves investment of time and effort in modeling and instructing new believers in the truths of the Christian faith. To effectively teach, we need to follow the example of the Master Teacher who took time to *"both to do and teach"* (Acts 1:1 NKJV).

Then too, the particular instruction to teach *"everything"* (Matthew 28:20) has particular relevance to the Church of today. We dare not be selective in our teaching. We must not neglect to give the full-orbed message of Christ. Christianity brings abiding joy, but it is not a joyride. Christianity brings peace, but it is also confrontational. Christianity brings hope, but it also presents the reality of lostness without Christ. Christianity brings freedom from all of sin's bondages, but it also warns us not to become re-entangled in sin's yoke.

> God desires ongoing fellowship with me and promises to be with me, empowering me to be His ambassador in a needy world.

Finally, the message concludes with the most encouraging words: *"And surely I am with you always, to the very end of the age"* (Matthew 28:20). As we highlighted in chapter 3 and again in chapter 8, we have the immeasurable offer of His divine presence with us. That little preposition *with* has enormous implications. We are never alone. We are invited to participate in the amazing work of the Kingdom of God as a joint venture with the Lord Himself! This closing thought reinforces the theme of this writing—God desires ongoing fellowship with me and promises to be with me, empowering me to be His ambassador in a needy world.

"Come fill this temple afresh with your presence, Lord Jesus!"

Dear Lord, for too long I have taken a neutral stance and kept a guarded distance from the place of front-line engagement.

Forgive me for my reticence to move from my place of comfort. I know that my life will be fruitful in Your kingdom only as I become vulnerable and willing to venture into areas where I must rely completely on You.

I ask that You would send a revival throughout our land, but until You descend in revival fire among us, teach me to be faithful to the task You've given Your Church. Give me a heart that is moved with compassion and filled with faith to see lives restored, the lost redeemed, and the souls of people filled with the hope that You alone can give.

Let me see the world through Your eyes and let me bring gladness to Your heart by reaching those You came to save. Through Your mercy, and in Your name, I pray.

Amen.

Epilogue

A S I'VE READ AND REREAD THE MANUSCRIPT, I HAVE BEEN deeply moved. My emotions have run the gamut from gratitude for my heritage to concern for the spiritual well-being of the succeeding generation, to rejoicing in the rediscovered relevance of ancient truths, to profoundly appreciating Christ's personal call and the pursuant blessings on my life. What incredible love He has lavished upon me that I should know His Spirit's leading and ongoing ministry in my life! It is so frighteningly easy to grow accustomed to His truth and His presence and to take it all for granted. My prayer for you, the reader, is that a renewed hunger for the nearness of His presence would overtake you and that together we might intently seek the Lord's face.

Another song from my youth comes immediately to mind, and it goes like this:

> O take me back to Calvary
> Where first I saw Thy face,
> Where Thou didst freely pardon me
> And save me by Thy grace.

Simple and yet profound, this song would be recognized by many of my generation. It could easily be written off as simplistic and lacking in originality or imagination. Yet my firm conviction is that we would do well to allow the Spirit of the Lord to impact our souls afresh with the need to acquire a new appreciation for the cleansing, purifying, restoring work of the cross in our lives.

Even though we have touched on revivalism in the course of our journey, I don't feel any compulsion to probe the dynamics of revival theology. I simply need to become reacquainted with the beauty of the matchless Christ and the wonder of His love for me. The journey up the various mountains has stirred in me a new dedication to His truth and a hunger for His presence.

It's been worth the effort for me to again value the truths and principles that were instilled in me from my earliest days. I marvel at how effective my parents were in laying an unshakeable foundation for the building blocks of my life. Because these truths have been foundational, I, along with countless others, see that souls can be rescued and society transformed only through the proclamation and the living out of the dynamics of the Christ in-dwelt, Spirit-empowered life.

Reading the manuscript again before preparing the final copy to be sent to the publisher, I was sitting across the table from Brenda, having coffee. She said to me, "I think what you need to say by way of conclusion is said right here." She was reading *My Heart's Cry,* by Anne Graham Lotz.

As I have pored over the Scriptures, my heart has cried out for more than just enough...

to escape a fiery hell.
to be saved from God's wrath.
to call myself a Christian.
to manage my guilt.
to get a ticket to heaven.
to squeak through heaven's gate.

I long for more than the bare minimum God has to offer.
I long for more than what the average Christian seems to settle for.
I long for everything God wants to give me.
I long for more than enough...

to bend my will!
to awaken my conscience!
to break my heart!
to transform my mind!
to overcome my prejudices!
to soar in my spirit!
to conform me to His glorious image!
to give me an abundant entrance into heaven!

I long to be saturated in Jesus! *So, please, dear God, just give me more...*[42]

Brenda understood what I needed to express. She was right!

Endnotes

1 Josh McDowell, "Rebuilding the Foundations," interview with Phil Callaway, *Servant Magazine*, Spring 2006, www.christianity.ca/family/parenting/2006/06.001.html.

2 John Phillips, *The View From Mount Calvary* (Grand Rapids: Kregel Publications, 2006), 30.

3 Henry Blackaby, *Created to be God's Friend: Lessons from the Life of Abraham* (Nashville: Thomas Nelson Publishers, 1999), 164.

4 Ron Sider, *The Scandal of the Evangelical Conscience* (Grand Rapids: Baker Books, 2005), 28.

5 Mark Buchanan, *The Rest of God* (Nashville: W. Publishing Group, 2006), 220.

6 Leonard Ravenhill, *Why Revival Tarries* (Minnesota: Bethany House Publishers, 1983), 69.

7 Thoro Harris, "He's Coming Soon," circa 1918, www.cyberhymnal.org/htm/h/e/hescomin.htm.

8 Randy Alcorn, *Heaven* (Wheaton: Tyndale House Publishers, 2004), 17.

9 Ibid.

10 Charles H. Gabriel, "O That Will Be Glory," *Hymns of Glorious Praise* (Springfield, MO: Gospel Publishing House, 1969), 152.

11 Fanny Crosby, "My Savior First of All," *Hymns of Glorious Praise* (Springfield, MO: Gospel Publishing House, 1969), 151.

12 Mercy Me, "I Can Only Imagine," www.lyricsdownload.com/mercy-me-i-can-only-imagine-lyrics.html.

13 John Stott, "Why Don't They Listen?" interview with Gary Barnes, *ChristianityToday*, September 1, 2003, www.ctlibrary.com/10879.

14 "Born Again Christians," The Barna Group, http://www.barna.org/FlexPage.aspx?Page=Topic&TopicID=8.

15 "Americans Draw Theological Beliefs From Diverse Points of View," The Barna Group, October 8, 2002, www.barna.org/FlexPage.aspx?Page=BarnaUpdate&BarnaUpdateID=122.

16 John Stott, "Why Don't They Listen?"

17 Josh McDowell and David H. Bellis, *The Last Christian Generation* (Holiday, FL: Green Key Books, 2006), 15.

18 Judson Cornwall, *Let Us Worship* (Plainfield, NJ: Bridge Publishing Co. 1983), 87.

19 Oswald J. Smith, *The Peoples Hymns, The Glory of His Presence* ed. David E. Williams (Toronto: The Peoples Press, 1978), 135.

20 Ibid., "For Me to Live Is Christ," 148.

21 Ravi Zacharias, *Walking from East to West* (Grand Rapids: Zondervan, 2006), 223.

22 Greg Paul, *God in the Alley* (Colorado Springs: Waterbrook Press), 2005, 30.

23 Tim Stafford, " Mere Mission," *Christianity Today*, January 2007, 41.

24 Charles Wesley, "And Can It Be That I Should Gain?" *Psalms and Hymns* (1738), http://www.cyberhymnal.org/htm/a/c/acanitbe.htm.

25 K. W. Osbeck, *Amazing Grace: 366 Inspiring Hymn Stories For Daily Devotions*, Grand Rapids: Kregel Publications, 1990, 107

26 Alfred H. Ackley, "Take Up Thy Cross" (1922), www.cyberhymnal.org/htm/t/u/tutcross.htm.

27 Mary Brown, "I'll Go Where You Want Me to Go," *Our Best Endeavor* (Silver Burdett and Company: 1892), www.cyberhymnal.org/htm/i/g/igowhere.htm.

28 John M. Moore, *My Songs and Their Stories* (Stouffville, Canada: John M. Moore Music, Inc., 2003), 49.

29 K. W. Osbeck.

30 Isaac Watts, "When I Survey the Wondrous Cross," *Hymns and Spiritual Songs* (1707), www.cyberhymnal.org/htm/w/h/e/whenisur.htm.

31 Colin N. Peckham, *Heritage of Revival* (Edinburgh: The Faith Mission, 1986), 93.

32 Duncan Campbell, "When the Mountains Flowed Down," members.aol.com/thewaycm/revival/campbell.html.

33 Ibid.

34 "The Hebrides Revival 1949," members.aol.com/thewaycm/revival/hebredies.html.

35 Ibid.

36 Isaac Watts and Robert Lowry, "Marching to Zion," *Hymns and Spiritual Songs* (1707), www.cyberhymnal.org/htm/m/a/marching.htm.

37 John W. Thompson and Randy Scruggs, "Sanctuary," www.pwarchive.com/song.aspx?SongID=145&v=1.

38 Thomas Wm. Miller, *Ripe for Revival: The Churches at the Crossroads of Renewal or Decline* (Burlington, ON: Welch Publishing Company, 1984), 177.

39 Henry Blackaby, *Experiencing God* (Nashville: Broadman and Holman Publishers, 1994), 82.

40 Charles Price and Elizabeth McQuoid, *Connect with the Heart of God: Hebrews* (Waynesboro, GA: Authentic Media, 2004), 48.

41 Oswald J. Smith, *The Passion for Souls* (Toronto: Evangelical Publishers), 1965. 75.

42 Anne Graham Lotz, *My Heart's Cry* (Nashville: W Publishing Group, 2002), xiii.

Order Information

**For more information and/or to order
additional copies of Timber and Timber Study Guide,
please contact:**
SummitPublications.org
info@summitpublications.org

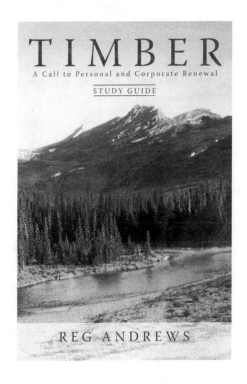